W9-CEI-875

HALLUCINOGENS

DRUG
EDUCATION
LIBRARY

HALLUCINOGENS

by James Barter

DRUG
EDUCATION
LIBRARY

Lucent Books, San Diego, CA

Library of Congress Cataloging-in-Publication Data

Barter, James, 1946–
   Hallucinogens / by James Barter.
     p.   cm. — (Drug education library)
Includes bibliographical references and index.
Summary: Discusses the development of hallucinogens,
their use for spiritual, medicinal, and recreational
purposes, and the laws governing their use.
   ISBN 1-56006-915-5 (hardback : alk. paper)
   1. Hallucinogenic drugs—Juvenile literature.
2. Hallucinogenic plants—Juvenile literature.
[1. Hallucinogenic drugs. 2. Drugs. 3. Drug abuse.]
I. Title. II. Series.
   HV5822 .H25 B37 2002
   362.29'4—dc21

2001005776

Contents

Foreword

The development of drugs and drug use in America is a cultural paradox. On the one hand, strong, potentially dangerous drugs provide people with relief from numerous physical and psychological ailments. Sedatives like Valium counter the effects of anxiety; steroids treat severe burns, anemia, and some forms of cancer; morphine provides quick pain relief. On the other hand, many drugs (sedatives, steroids, and morphine among them) are consistently misused or abused. Millions of Americans struggle each year with drug addictions that overpower their ability to think and act rationally. Researchers often link drug abuse to criminal activity, traffic accidents, domestic violence, and suicide.

These harmful effects seem obvious today. Newspaper articles, medical papers, and scientific studies have highlighted the myriad problems drugs and drug use can cause. Yet, there was a time when many of the drugs now known to be harmful were actually believed to be beneficial. Cocaine, for example, was once hailed as a great cure, used to treat everything from nausea and weakness to colds and asthma. Developed in Europe during the 1880s, cocaine spread quickly to the United States where manufacturers made it the primary ingredient in such everyday substances as cough medicines, lozenges, and tonics. Likewise, heroin, an opium derivative, became a popular painkiller during the late nineteenth century. Doctors and patients flocked to American drugstores to buy heroin, described as the optimal cure for even the worst coughs and chest pains.

As more people began using these drugs, though, doctors, legislators, and the public at large began to realize that they were more damaging than beneficial. After years of using heroin as a painkiller, for example, patients began asking their doctors for larger and stronger doses. Cocaine users reported dangerous side effects, including hallucinations and wild mood shifts. As a result, the U.S. government initiated more stringent regulation of many powerful and addictive drugs, and in some cases outlawed them entirely.

A drug's legal status is not always indicative of how dangerous it is, however. Some drugs known to have harmful effects can be purchased legally in the United States and elsewhere. Nicotine, a key ingredient in cigarettes, is known to be highly addictive. In an effort to meet their bodies' demands for nicotine, smokers expose themselves to lung cancer, emphysema, and other life-threatening conditions. Despite these risks, nicotine is legal almost everywhere.

Other drugs that cannot be purchased or sold legally are the subject of much debate regarding their effects on physical and mental health. Marijuana, sometimes described as a gateway drug that leads users to other drugs, cannot legally be used, grown, or sold in this country. However, some research suggests that marijuana is neither addictive nor a gateway drug and that it might actually benefit cancer and AIDS patients by reducing pain and encouraging failing appetites. Despite these findings and occasional legislative attempts to change the drug's status, marijuana remains illegal.

The Drug Education Library examines the paradox of drugs and drug use in America by focusing on some of the most commonly used and abused drugs or categories of drugs available today. By discussing objectively the many types of drugs, their intended purposes, their effects (both planned and unplanned), and the controversies surrounding them, the books in this series provide readers with an understanding of the complex role drugs and drug use play in American society. Informative sidebars, annotated bibliographies, and organizations to contact lists highlight the text and provide young readers with many opportunities for further discussion and research.

 **Introduction**

The Resurgence of Hallucinogens

H allucinogens are ancient drugs. They have been used for thousands of years in religious ceremonies, as sources of inspiration for artists, as medicines, and of course for some simply as a means of altering their perceptions of the physical world. In America, although the consumption of certain hallucinogens has been a part of religious practice among native peoples for many generations, to the general public, the decade of the 1960s is most closely linked with these drugs, popularly called psychedelics. During this decade, widespread experimentation with LSD, peyote, and "magic mushrooms" influenced many aspects of American pop culture. San Francisco emerged as the mecca for psychedelic "love-ins," beatnik poetry readings, and music called acid rock and psychedelic rock. The image of long-haired hippies wearing beads and tie-dyed clothes and speaking in psychedelic-influenced language is etched in popular memory. Many people flocked to hear the guru of LSD, Timothy Leary, urge everyone in San Francisco's Golden Gate Park to take the opportunity to experience hallucinogens' weird effects firsthand.

Thanks in part to the advice of Leary and others, the 1960s was a decade of unprecedented psychedelic drug use. The Haight-Ashbury district in San Francisco and Telegraph Avenue in Berkeley became twin casbahs for the sale or trade of every known hallucinogen. Thousands of restless young Americans flocked to northern California to participate in what became a sort of drug revolution. No one knew how these enigmatic drugs caused their psychedelic trips, and few users took the time to be concerned.

For most Americans today, hallucinogens seem mostly to belong to this bygone era. However, statistics provided by governmental health and law enforcement agencies suggest that, although there was a decrease in hallucinogen use during the '70s and '80s, the '90s saw a resurgence of these drugs that continues into the twenty-first century. The nation's experience with LSD serves as an example. According to the National Institute on Drug Abuse, the lifetime use of LSD among high school seniors nationwide was at its lowest in 1986 at 7.2 percent, but in 1999 the number of high school seniors who reported having ever tried LSD nearly doubled to 14.2 percent. Other surveys report different numbers, but the upward trend in the use of LSD is still apparent. According to the National Household Survey on Drug

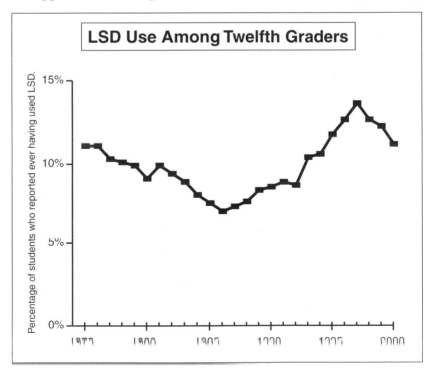

Abuse, the percentage of seniors reporting use of LSD doubled from a low of 4.4 percent in 1985 to 8.7 percent in 1999.

If the use of hallucinogens such as LSD has surged, the use of new hallucinogens such as ecstasy and ketamine, associated with the 1990s rave culture, has exploded. For example, according to estimates compiled by the Drug Enforcement Administration (DEA), the quantity of illicit ecstasy pills on the streets of the United States rose from 360,000 in 1985 to more than 100 million.

The debate that swirls around the use of hallucinogens in America has many aspects. Uncertainties such as how hallucinogens work in the brain, whether they pose a long-term health risk, and whether they place the morals of the nation in peril have sparked pockets of public debate regarding their legal status. Presently, the possession or sale of most hallucinogens without a permit from the Food and Drug Administration is a felony. Although the majority of Americans continue to support the legal ban on hallucinogens, many others believe there are reasons to revisit the regulations on a drug-by-drug basis.

The controversy surrounding the use and legality of hallucinogens is complex and emotionally charged. No one group or person holds the decisive answer. Nevertheless, as the use of hallucinogens continues to rise regardless of their outlaw status, individuals both in and out of government continue to research and discuss this issue of modifying the nation's drug policy, and the debate shows no sign of subsiding.

 **Chapter 1**

A Strange Class of Drugs

Hallucinogens are drugs that, when ingested, trigger a variety of strange and unpredictable sensations and experiences. Normally, such bizarre perceptions are experienced only in dreams, during periods of extreme emotional and physical stress, or as part of severe mental disorders such as schizophrenia.

Psychoactive Chemicals

There are dozens of different types of hallucinogens, some of which are produced naturally by plants and some of which are synthesized in laboratories or other facilities. There are many different hallucinogens used today, but the best known are mescaline and psilocybin, which come from plants, and LSD, ecstasy, and ketamine, which are manufactured in laboratories. What these drugs have in common is an ability to alter the functioning of the brain in such a way as to either modify the user's perceptions or create entirely artificial perceptions. Users of hallucinogens experience a range of odd sensations, from mild distortions of information affecting the senses of sight, hearing, smell, taste, and touch to highly animated and dramatic sensory distortions—the hallucinations that give this class of drugs its name.

Altered Perceptions

Typically, users of hallucinogens characterize these sensations as seeing unusually vivid colors, hearing music with unusual clarity, tasting
flavors never before experienced in foods, and smelling aromas of
food with enough intensity to trigger eating binges. Users may find
everyday experiences intensely funny or sad, and find mundane objects such as kitchen appliances fascinating, as though they are being
experienced for the first time. Sometimes, personal experiences can
seem to be more profound and offer greater insight than had been
the case in the past. One user interviewed by researchers reported
what he experienced while under the influence of a hallucinogen:

> At one point, we went outside, it was dark out by now, and I remember look-
> ing at the street, and being aware of how the street sparkled. I had never no-
> ticed this before. Then I looked at the sky, and it looked like dark blue foil, sort
> of like foil wrapping paper, not the shiny kind, but the matte, etched kind. . . . I
> remember also becoming extremely aware of tactile changes. There was a gen-
> tle breeze that night. I felt the breeze kiss my skin. . . . I almost felt as though I
> had been touched by God. I felt like I was being enveloped by all of nature.[1]

*Users often report that their senses are heightened after the consumption of
LSD.*

These types of sensory alterations are considered mild, and they tend to occur when people take low doses of a hallucinogen. When people take larger doses, these alterations occur early in what is commonly called a "trip"—the hallucinogenic experience—but these are often followed by more dramatic and intense phenomena: actual hallucinations.

Hallucinations

Unlike altered perceptions, which are triggered by some sort of external stimulus, hallucinations are sensations that people experience when there is no external stimulus. A hallucination can be experienced through any of the five senses. Hallucinations can sometimes be dramatic and complex, and as a result they can be quite frightening.

Those who have taken large doses of hallucinogens often report experiencing bizarre and impossible events. For example, some users witness inanimate objects or people morphing into animals, objects talking and moving around a room, or extraterrestrial beings visiting from outer space. Others claim to have interactions with dead people.

As bizarre as these drug-induced hallucinations can be, there are some features of hallucinations that are commonly experienced. Users often report walls flexing back and forth to the rhythm of music, straight lines curving and then straightening out, and objects appearing and then disappearing from view. In an interview, a college student recalled this LSD experience:

> We went to the sink that had little droplets of water in the bottom of it. By "unfocusing" our attention, we could cause strange effects to occur. The sink became this rushing current of rapids pouring down into the drain. A blink of the eyes and it was the sink again. . . . There was a poster around campus that week for a band known as Anonymous. . . . It was a picture of a punk rocker's face with really strange shadings that had obvious [sic] been done with pencil. We watched the poster for a moment. The hair on the top of his head receded and disappeared while the shading on the face became more pronounced turning the face into that of a "wolfman.". . . The face cycled back and forth between that of the punk rocker and the wolfman, back and forth like the waves on the shore. . . . The kitchen was full of wonders. The doors on all the shelves bulged inward and outward. The hairs on our arms interweaved continually and the hairs on our legs grew straight out. The once plain walls were full of intricate little patterns as was the carpet.[2]

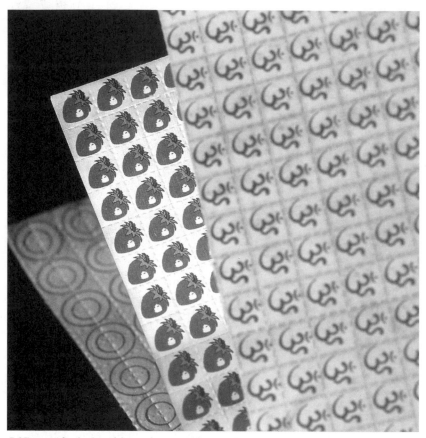

LSD can be infused into sheets of blotting paper and is released when the paper is placed in the mouth.

Users of these drugs claim that they usually understand during their trip that the hallucinations are drug induced and that the bizarre experience will soon end. In this sense, they are very different from dreams or hallucinations induced by extreme stress.

Another common feature of hallucinogens is that many users also claim to have gained new religious insights as a result of their trips. Many report finding new purposes for their lives, a sense that all people, animals, and objects are spiritually connected, and some establish an emotional identification with one or more of history's great spiritual leaders, such as Jesus or Buddha. One writer expressed these spiritual thoughts following an experience with mescaline:

I began to feel like I was so connected with all of life and nature. I think, at that moment, I never felt more alive. I think somehow during this trip, I also became more aware of my own immortality. I seem to remember thinking about dying, and for the first time, it didn't really scare me because I seemed to be aware that my soul somehow transcended anything physical. I felt very thankful that God had put me on earth to see beauty.[3]

Despite the common elements reported by those who have used hallucinogens, drug-induced hallucinations are highly unpredictable. The experience one has with the drug may be pleasurable one time and highly disturbing the next, or, as is sometimes the case with LSD, over the course of a single trip, both pleasurable and frightening elements can occur. Occasionally, the frightening effects of hallucinogens can intensify, causing the affected person to experience feelings of hopelessness and intense anxiety that persist long after the drug itself has left the body. If this depression does not subside, people have been known to behave in ways that endanger their lives. Such out-of-control behaviors occasionally require at least short-term hospitalization.

Hallucinogens and the Brain

Although the bizarre and fanciful effects of some hallucinogens have been known for thousands of years, it is only within the last fifty years that scientists have begun to unravel the mystery of how these drugs work. Researchers now believe that chemicals called neurotransmitters, which are produced in the brain, are responsible for the eerie sensory fabrications associated with hallucinogens.

Neurotransmitters are naturally occurring chemical compounds that transmit signals between the brain's neurons. There is a microscopic gap between the neurons called a synapse, which signals must cross in order for information to pass from one neuron to another. For a signal to move along, each synapse must be temporarily bridged by a neurotransmitter. Then, within milliseconds after the message has been passed, the neurotransmitter withdraws from the synapse back into the neurons in a process called re-uptake; the synapse empties once again and awaits the next signal.

In the presence of certain drugs, including hallucinogens, the re-uptake process fails, causing abnormally high concentrations of neurotransmitters to build up in the synapses. When this occurs, the brain begins to behave abnormally. Researchers have identified more than fifty neurotransmitters, but they believe that one, serotonin, is the neurotransmitter that builds up in the presence of the psychoactive chemicals found in hallucinogens. Serotonin is known to affect a person's moods, memory, sleep, body temperature, and general behavior. Since each person has only about ten milligrams of serotonin, a small increase can significantly alter the function of the brain. Therefore, even a small amount of a hallucinogen can produce what experts call an altered state of consciousness.

Serotonin is not, however, found in equal amounts throughout the brain. Neurologists believe that serotonin figures most prominently in

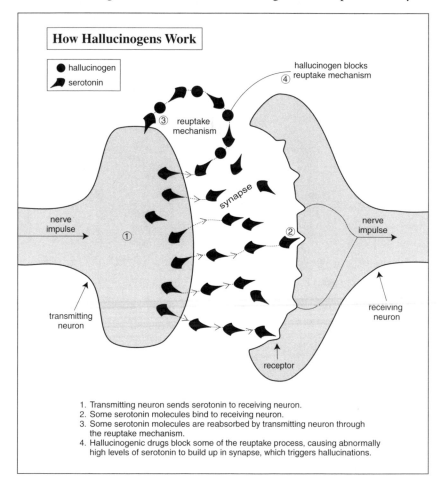

How Hallucinogens Work

● hallucinogen
🢡 serotonin

④ hallucinogen blocks reuptake mechanism

③ reuptake mechanism

synapse

nerve impulse
①

②

nerve impulse

transmitting neuron

receiving neuron

receptor

1. Transmitting neuron sends serotonin to receiving neuron.
2. Some serotonin molecules bind to receiving neuron.
3. Some serotonin molecules are reabsorbed by transmitting neuron through the reuptake mechanism.
4. Hallucinogenic drugs block some of the reuptake process, causing abnormally high levels of serotonin to build up in synapse, which triggers hallucinations.

two brain regions: one is the cerebral cortex, an area involved in thought, mood, and perception; the other is the locus coeruleus, which receives sensory signals from all areas of the body and has been described as the brain's device for identifying novelty among external stimuli. This would help explain how the increased levels of serotonin could lead to the bizarre sensory experiences reported by users of hallucinogens.

It is worth noting that this view of how these drugs work in the brain is still theoretical. As Dr. Solomon Snyder of Johns Hopkins University writes,

> Again, *we do not know for certain* exactly how the brain regulates specific behaviors, but we can formulate some educated guesses and . . . we can use these guesses as the basis for the next important advances in understanding.[4]

Physical Effects

In addition to the perceptual distortions caused by hallucinogens, commonly experienced physiological reactions include dilated pupils, lowered body temperature, nausea, profuse sweating, goose bumps, and occasionally, rapid heartbeat and elevated blood pressure.

Despite these well-documented physical effects, medical researchers are nearly unanimous in their belief that, although hallucinogens can produce some short-term physical changes in the brain, there seem to be very few, if any, long-term or permanent changes when used in moderate dosages by healthy users. Perhaps for this reason, death caused by toxic effects of most hallucinogens is unknown in scientific literature. However, injuries and deaths as a result of dangerous and irrational behavior while under the influence of hallucinogens have occurred. In addition, extremely large doses of some hallucinogens, or mixing several different drugs, can pose serious health risks and have been known to be fatal.

Addiction

Although most neurologists and pharmacologists report few lasting adverse physical effects from hallucinogen use, one concern among those who formulate the government's drug policies is whether hallucinogens might be addictive.

Of the scientific studies that have focused on this aspect of hallucinogens, none has concluded that they are addictive. This means that their prolonged use does not create a physiological craving or dependency based on changes in a user's body chemistry. In addition, unlike drugs known to be addictive, there do not appear to be any physiological withdrawal symptoms or cravings when use of hallucinogens is terminated.

Furthermore, unlike users of addictive drugs, users of hallucinogens typically do not have the urge to take their drugs many times a day. In fact, hallucinogenic experiences tend to be exhausting, and users report needing time to rest and recover following a trip. The use of hallucinogens more often than once a week is extremely rare; the majority of regular users report using them once a month or a few sporadic times in the course of a year. One of the reasons given for this low frequency of use is the long duration of a hallucinogen trip, which often lasts many hours. The effects of addictive drugs, in comparison, wear off more quickly.

In addition to not being addictive, hallucinogens do not appear to build tolerance in users. As a result, the dose level of hallucinogens tends to remain constant. There is little motivation for increasing dosages. Although higher doses of hallucinogens will increase perceptual distortions and the intensity of hallucinations, many users report that they do not feel comfortable when a trip gets out of control. Plus, users typically do not feel the need to increase their dosage over time to achieve the same effect, as is often the case with addictive drugs. In fact, quite the opposite is true. The Drug Enforcement Administration (DEA) reports, for example, that the typical dose of LSD has declined from an average of 250 micrograms during the 1960s to about 100 micrograms today.

The position taken by most researchers, that hallucinogens are not addictive, is supported by the National Institute on Drug Abuse (NIDA), which published this statement regarding LSD: "Most users of LSD voluntarily decrease or stop its use over time. LSD is not considered an addictive drug since it does not produce compulsive drug-seeking behavior as do cocaine, amphetamine, heroin, alcohol, and nicotine."[5] The NIDA and the DEA make similar comments about other hallucinogens as well.

The Pineal Gland

Recent research is tentatively pointing to the pineal gland as holding the answer to the question "How do some hallucinogens such as mescaline, psilocybin, and LSD alter perceptions more dramatically than other hallucinogens?"

Early researchers believed that the pineal, about the size of a grain of rice and shaped like a pine cone and located in the center of the brain, served a purpose millions of years ago but had long since ceased to be of any use. In 1958, however, a Yale Medical School professor named Aaron B. Lerner dissected 250,000 pineal glands from cattle and discovered that they are a source of serotonin, the same neurotransmitter that neurologists believe is responsible for mood changes and altered states of perception in humans.

Lerner's colleagues later continued his research by examining the brains of human cadavers and discovered that different areas of the human brain store varying amounts of serotonin. However, of all the sources of serotonin in the human brain, the pineal was unmistakably the richest.

The connection between hallucinogens and elevated levels of serotonin as the probable explanation for dramatic mood shifts and hallucinations has been well received by researchers even though it is still considered theoretical. If it is correct, then it may follow that the more potent hallucinogens have the unique ability to stimulate the pineal to release its relatively large reservoir of serotonin which in turn causes the dramatic altered states reported by LSD users.

Most researchers believe that hallucinogens cause the pineal gland (highlighted) to release serotonin, resulting in an altered state of consciousness.

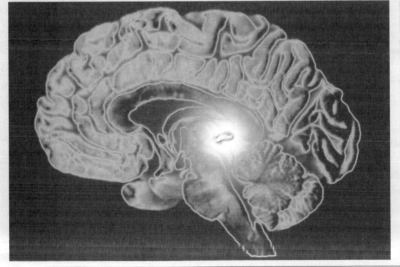

Psychedelic Rock

The influence of psychedelic drugs during the 1960s flooded the music world. Many of the best-known singers and songwriters produced hit after hit record with lyrics reflecting the drug culture. This musical style was invented in San Francisco by groups using surreal and mystical imagery inspired by psychedelic experiences. It was intended to be played while under the influence of psychedelics.

Songs that directly referred to illicit drugs were banned on most radio stations, forcing writers to hide drug references in the lyrics. One of the most famous psychedelic songs with surreptitious images associated with the altered perceptions of hallucinogens was the song "White Rabbit" by the Jefferson Airplane. This song describes taking pills that distort perceptions while talking to animals that are behaving as though they are people.

The Beatles were one of the most prolific recorders of psychedelic songs. In their song "Tomorrow Never Knows," they use mystical spiritual imagery common to the drug culture of the 1960s to describe a dreamy relaxation while floating on a river contemplating the mysteries of life.

Possibly the most widely celebrated example of hidden references to hallucinogens was the Beatles' song "Lucy in the Sky with Diamonds." The use of trancelike psychedelic imagery in the song was apparent to nearly everyone, but the real convincing clue to its hidden meaning was in its title: Many people believed that the L in "Lucy," the S in "Sky," and the D in "Diamonds" were a reference to LSD. Even though the Beatles denied that they had intentionally included a reference to LSD in their song, few listeners believed them.

Risks

Being nonaddictive does not mean hallucinogens are risk-free, however. Although the probability of death from the effects of a hallucinogen itself is low in comparison to narcotics such as heroin, health-care professionals warn that using hallucinogens can still have serious health consequences. There are no known deaths among humans because of brain, heart, or pulmonary failure that can be directly attributed to an overdose of any hallucinogen (although laboratory animals administered high doses of LSD have died from respiratory arrest). However, even though studies indicate that low doses of hallucinogens produce no long-lasting effects, high doses of hallucinogens have been known to cause severe psychotic breakdowns requiring long periods of psychiatric treatment.

The danger of hallucinogens lies not in their toxicity but, rather, in the unpredictability of their psychological effects. For example, users have been known to wander down streets without knowing who they are or where they have been, or have walked in freezing weather without proper clothing, unaware that they were suffering from frostbite.

Episodes of fatal consequences of hallucinogen use, mostly attributed to LSD, have been recorded. Pedestrians under the influence of LSD have been killed when they wandered into busy streets. There have also been reports of LSD users committing suicide because of the disorienting effects of the drug. Doctors Martin H. Keeler and Clifford B. Reifler reported the suicide of a twenty-year-old college student who completely disrobed and jumped from a window to his death while under the influence of LSD. In the article they wrote describing the student's mental state before the suicide, the doctors concluded: "The circumstances strongly suggest that he would not have died at the time he did if he were not in a state of LSD intoxication."[6]

Coroner reports tend to support the anecdotal evidence that hallucinogens such as LSD, mescaline, and psilocybin (also known as "magic mushrooms") are relatively nontoxic. Between 1994 and 1998, for example, the Drug Abuse Warning Network (DAWN) reported an average of two deaths per year relating to LSD, none for peyote, and none for magic mushrooms. In cases where deaths have occurred, most coroner reports of victims' blood samples reveal the presence of multiple drugs, rarely just one. The nation's health reports indicate that the most common cause of death among hallucinogen users occurs from mixing hallucinogens with other drugs, especially with alcohol. Alcohol functions as a depressant that can suppress the breathing reflexes and in the presence of hallucinogens, which disorient the brain, the body's natural response to increase breathing can be obstructed.

Illness or deaths have also resulted from hallucinogens that are contaminated with toxic substances. Health officials point out that, because no government or health agency regulates the manufacturing of illegal drugs, ingesting a pill supposedly containing a hallucinogen is often an act of faith on the part of the user. Hallucinogens cannot be tested for purity except in a laboratory with sophisticated equipment—rarely an

option for casual users. As a result, the first indication that a toxic cont-
aminant is present may well be the sudden severe reaction or death of
the user.

Even when the dosage and purity of a drug are known, some risk
remains. This is because heredity plays a significant role in an individ-

Hallucinogens: False Prophets

Some writers and artists who advocated the use of hallucino-gens during the 1960s later re-canted their views. Writer Ken Kesey was one of the first to dis-avow his earlier opinions. Nov-elist Tom Wolfe quotes Kesey in *The Electric Kool-Aid Acid Test*: "What I told the hippies was that LSD can be a door that one uses to open his mind to new realms of experience, but many hippies are using it just to keep going through the door over and over again, without trying to learn anything from it."

Richard Alpert, who researched LSD and advocated its use in collaboration with Timothy Leary at Harvard University, said in a 1970 interview with *Play-boy* magazine, "I think LSD is making itself obsolete. All acid does is show you the possibil-ity of another type of con-

Novelist Peter Matthiessen believes that hallucinogens are not the magic formula for personal growth.

sciousness and give you hope. But your own impurities keep bringing you down. . . . After a while you dig that if you want to *stay high*, you have to work on yourself."

Novelist and adventurer Peter Matthiessen, who experimented with hallu-cinogens for a time, had this comment about how drugs affect the mind in his book *Snow Leopard:* "Drugs cannot clear away the past and enhance the present; toward the inner garden, they can only point the way. Lacking the grit of discipline and insight, the drug vision remains a sort of dream that cannot be brought over into daily life. Old mists may be banished, that is true, but the alien chemical agent forms another mist, maintaining the separation of the 'I' from true experience of the infinite within us."

ual's reaction to hallucinogens. For example, the probability of experiencing long-term psychological harm from hallucinogens increases among users who have a hereditary predisposition to psychotic behavior such as schizophrenia. Heredity also determines an individual's natural amount of serotonin, which can vary. Researchers speculate that users who experience dangerously out-of-control hallucinations have inherited naturally occurring levels of serotonin that are higher than those who experience milder hallucinations. Since few, if any, people know their natural level of serotonin, there is no way to predict whether someone will experience a severe adverse reaction or none at all—particularly the first time they try a hallucinogen.

Regardless of the risks posed by taking hallucinogens, they are used by millions of people. In fact, hallucinogens are so important in some cultures that their use is considered sacred.

Chapter 2

Hallucinogens and Spiritual Rituals

For thousands of years, people in many cultures have used hallucinogens in an attempt to gain spiritual insights to help them deal with the uncertainties that are part of their daily lives. They try to communicate with their deities to gain understanding and control over unpredictable events like birth, death, and illness. People in these cultures induce hallucinations by eating plants such as peyote and several species of mushrooms that naturally produce hallucinogenic chemicals. Botanists and ethnologists who have studied this use of hallucinogens refer to psychoactive plants used in religious rituals as entheogens, from the Greek word meaning "divinely inspired."

Ancient Use

Archaeologists believe that hallucinogens were also used in a number of ancient societies to help leaders make important decisions relating to issues such as war, hunting, migrating to a new home, and selecting tribal and spiritual leaders. All of these situations were important enough to require consultation with a deity, who was believed to communicate with earthly beings while they were in a trance.

Why entheogens were used in religious rituals in the first place is uncertain. But scholars studying these ancient cultures have a plausible answer to this question. They generally believe that the altered perceptions experienced by those ingesting the entheogens were so extraordinary that ancient peoples believed they must have been inspired by the gods they worshiped. Some anthropologists speculate that those who took the drug believed that, by doing so, they were becoming acquainted with the gods themselves. This view is supported by ethnologist Richard Evans Schultes, who also notes that these entheogens soon were controlled by tribal religious leaders:

> When the unearthly and inexplicably weird physical and psychic effects of these few plants were experienced, it did not take long for primitive societies to regard them as sacred elements of the flora, and their use eventually fell into the province of the shamans or medicine men who explained their effects as proof that these species were the home of spirits or spiritual forces enabling man through various hallucinations to communicate with ancestors or with spirits in the outer realms.[7]

The Historical and Archaeological Record

The archaeological evidence of such use dates back between seven and nine thousand years and is found in most regions of the world.

For centuries peyote has been eaten as part of certain religious rituals.

For example, a cache of dried peyote, the hallucinogenic cactus, was found in a cave in Texas and has been carbon-dated to approximately 5000 B.C. Archaeologists have also located dozens of cave paintings and stone sculptures in Africa, Asia, and South America depicting hallucinogenic mushrooms and other plants. According to ethnologist Giorgio Samorini,

> The idea that the use of hallucinogens should be a source of inspiration for some forms of prehistoric rock art is not a new one. . . . Rock paintings [exist] in the Sahara Desert, the works of pre-neolithic Early Gatherers, in which mushrooms [sic] effigies are represented repeatedly. The polychromatic scenes of harvest, adoration and the offering of mushrooms, and large masked "gods" covered with mushrooms, not to mention other significant details, lead us to suppose we are dealing with an ancient hallucinogenic mushroom cult . . . and that their use always takes place within contexts and rituals of a religious nature.[8]

The earliest written records of the use of hallucinogenic drugs date back three thousand years. Writings from ancient civilizations throughout many regions of the world depict the use of entheogens as part of religious ceremonies.

For example, writings from the African Congo describe the Eboga plant used in rites-of-passage rituals for young men and women. The Eboga plant was pulled from the ground, the roots were cut off and scraped clean, and the fleshy part of the root eaten. The stories of those who ate the roots describe the "thunder" they felt in their heads, the dizziness, and the visions they experienced of people who were not actually present. Similarly, ancient Hindu scriptures called the Veda refer to a hallucinogenic drink called soma. There is archaeological evidence that suggests how this drink was made: Ceramic strainers have been unearthed at ancient Hindu shrines, and laboratory tests revealed traces of three different hallucinogenic plants native to India. Even historical records from ancient Athenians indicate that a mysterious drink called *kykeon*, which induced a trancelike state, was consumed during religious ceremonies known as the Eleusinian Mysteries.

Although anthropologists agree on the importance of hallucinogens in early religious ceremonies, they are divided in their opinions of how the discovery of certain plants' powers may have occurred. One group speculates that members of primitive tribes probably watched animals

The Eleusinian Mysteries

Three thousand years ago in Greece, a religious ceremony, known today as the Eleusinian Mysteries, was held every year. During the ceremony, a mysterious and sacred brew was drunk by initiates. The Mysteries were celebrated at Eleusis, a small city east of Athens, from around 1500 B.C. to the fourth century A.D. in honor of the goddess Demeter and her daughter Persephone.

As many as three thousand people each year could walk to Eleusis for the initiation. Many famous Greeks and Romans such as Aristotle, Sophocles, Plato, and Cicero made the walk. The celebration of the Mysteries began in the autumn, with four days of rites and festivities in Athens. On the fifth day, a solemn procession to Eleusis began, during which rites, sacrifices, and purifications took place.

On the sixth night, cloaked in secrecy, the climax of the Eleusinian ceremony took place in the inner sanctum of the temple, into which only priests and initiates could enter. Before the climax of the initiation, a sacred potion made of barley and mint called *kykeon* was administered. Ancient Greek writers who experienced the drink reported mystical insights into birth and death and strange ritualistic babbling.

The possible psychoactive ingredients in *kykeon* have been hotly debated. Botanists and anthropologists have made many suggestions, but the one most universally accepted is put forth by Gordon Wasson, Albert Hofmann, and Carl Ruck in their book *The Road to Eleusis*. These researchers believe that ergot, a type of fungus found on various grains, was the psychoactive component of *kykeon*. It would have been simple for an Eleusinian priest to collect the ergot, grind it into a powder, and add it to the *kykeon*. The theory is further supported by the fact that ergot is generally found on grain and Demeter was the goddess of the grain harvest who figured prominently in the ritual.

Most archaeologists and classical scholars, however, express great reluctance in accepting the ideas put forth in *The Road to Eleusis*. They tend to believe that, although there was a secret drink given to initiates during the Mysteries and the drink caused bizarre reactions, it remains a matter of speculation whether hallucinogens were part of the drink.

Telesterion, located near Athens and the site of the Eleusinian Mysteries ceremony, is where some archaeologists believe initiates were given a hallucinogenic drink known as kykeon.

eat various hallucinogenic plants and then observed their strange disori-
ented behaviors. Ethnologists further speculate that, at some point,
members of the tribe decided to eat the plants to experience the same
effect.

Other anthropologists believe that the discovery of the psychoactive plants must be attributed to simple experimentation with most or
all of the plants in the local environment. When those who sampled
new plants inexplicably experienced strange intoxicating effects, they
knew they had discovered a plant that provided something other than
nourishment.

Although many types of entheogens exist, the two that are best
known are various species of hallucinogenic cactus and mushrooms.

Entheogens as Spiritual Medicine

The most commonly reported ritual use of entheogens among indigenous peoples of the Western Hemisphere is for healing the sick.
Among such cultures, the world of medicine and the spirit world are
inseparable. Anthropologist Henry Munn writes that, among the
tribal peoples of the Mexican state of Oaxaca, the mushrooms are not
simply botanical hallucinogens; they "were known to the American
Indians as medicines. . . . Among the Mazatecs [an Oaxacan tribe],
many, one time or another during their lives, have eaten the mushrooms, either to cure themselves of an ailment or to resolve a problem."[9]

Each Oaxacan tribe has at least one shaman, similar to a medicine
man, who specializes in the use of hallucinogens for the purpose of
healing others. A shaman is recognized by the tribe as an expert in
these matters; he functions as a spiritual guide and spokesman for
the ill person. Shamans have long known that hallucinogens cannot
cure ailments such as broken bones, but they believe that hallucinogens can cure many other medical problems, including those with
no apparent physical cause.

The healing session takes the form of a meeting in which both the
shaman and his patient eat the entheogen. After an hour or so, when
the hallucinations begin, the shaman acts very much like a Western
doctor or psychiatrist might and asks the patient about the origins of
the illness. After the patient describes the history of the illness, the

shaman goes into a trace and chants about where to look for the cure for the disease. As an example, Henry Munn recorded this chant:

> My God, you who are the master of the whole world, what we want is to search for and encounter from where comes sickness, from where comes pain and affliction. We are the ones who speak and cure and use medicine. So without mishap, without difficulty, lift us into the heights and exalt us.[10]

Following the chant, the shaman talks about how the mushrooms will heal the illness. He then tells the patient that the mushrooms are working to cure him and that he or she will soon be well. The shaman does not touch the patient in any way, as a Western-style doctor would. Instead, during the hallucination, he visualizes that he is sucking the illness out of the patient. Munn interviewed a shaman and asked how he was able to heal the sick. The shaman answered that the mushrooms taught him "how to suck through space with a hollow tube of cane. To suck through space means that you who are seated there, I can draw the sickness out of you by suction from a distance."[11]

Mazatec shamans believe that, when they heal an illness, it is actually the mushrooms that perform the healing by inducing the hallucinations, inspiring an understanding of the illness, and directing their thoughts to cure the illness. This practice is often successful, perhaps because it instills in the patient confidence that he or she will recover; even doctors trained in Western medicine recognize such confidence as being an important factor in whether a patient recovers.

To illustrate the importance of faith in the power of mushrooms among indigenous peoples, Munn tells the story of an ill villager who went to a shaman because of a severe pain in his abdomen. The shaman's treatment did not relieve the pain, forcing the villager to seek treatment in a hospital. Upon examination by a medical doctor, it was determined that the villager needed an appendectomy. The inflamed appendix was removed, but the patient's condition worsened for no reason the doctor could discern. After several days watching his patient refuse to eat and express his wish to die, the doctor summoned the shaman to the hospital for a second mushroom ceremony. While hallucinating, the patient revealed that since a steel knife had cut into him, his soul had been so grievously violated that he was dying of shame. The shaman, listening to this story, told the man that it

Bernardino de Sahagún and the *Florentine Codex*

In the mid–sixteenth century, Spanish priest Bernardino de Sahagún traveled throughout Mexico and wrote about the Aztec culture, including their use of hallucinogenic mushrooms and peyote. Sahagún's accounts of his travels through Mexico are the earliest writings describing the use of entheogens.

In his account of his travels in 1559, titled the *Florentine Codex*, Sahagún recorded the first known account of a magic mushroom ceremony, which is quoted in a website called the Vaults of Erowid: "The first thing to be eaten at the feast were small black mushrooms that they called *nanacatl* [divine flesh], and bring on drunkenness, hallucinations and even lechery; they ate these before the dawn . . . with honey; and when they began to feel the effects, they

The illustrations are reproduced from the Paso y Troncoso color edition of the *Florentine Codex*, 1905-07.

Bernardino de Sahagún's work, the Florentine Codex, *contains the first known account of the use of hallucinogenic mushrooms.*

began to dance, some sang and others wept. . . . When the drunkenness of the mushrooms had passed, they spoke with one another of the visions they had seen."

Sahagún also witnessed and recorded peyote ceremonies. He estimated that the Chichimeca and Toltec Indians had been using peyote at least two thousand years before the arrival of the Spaniards. Sahagún referred to the use of the root "peiotl" by the Chichimeca Indians of Mexico. The two most commonly used names, "peyote" and "peyotl," are modifications of that ancient word.

Had the writings of Sahagún not been discovered by mid–twentieth-century European pharmaceutical researchers, much of the research and knowledge they accumulated might not exist today.

was the mushrooms that had actually cut him open, rearranged his insides, and had sewn him up again. The man immediately recovered and returned to his village believing that the mushrooms had actually performed the surgery and that his soul should not feel ashamed of what had happened.

Entheogens and Religious Practice

The use of entheogens continues today in large areas of the Western Hemisphere, including the United States. In many cases, this modern use goes beyond healing. The most widely used entheagen is peyote, a form of cactus, which is legally used by some members of Native American tribes living in the Southwest and among tribes throughout Mexico and South America.

This cactus, which has the scientific name *Lophophora williamsii,* is found in the hot, dry climates of the American Southwest and in Mexico. Peyote is recognizable by its small, round blue-green body, called a button, which barely protrudes one inch above the ground. Each button is about the diameter of a quarter and is covered by soft fuzz rather than the spines that typify most cacti. The ingredient in the peyote button that produces hallucinations is a chemical compound called mescaline. Between four and ten buttons are picked for a single 350-milligram dose.

The Peyote Ceremony

The peyote ceremonies of Southwest American tribes all tend to follow a similar archetype, although each has its own unique variations. The peyote ceremony continues to serve the same role it did in ancient times, whenever an occasion requires spiritual guidance. Generally, the reasons for such a gathering involve decisions affecting the whole community, such as selecting new tribal leaders, enacting new tribal laws, and determining the use of tribal lands. The ceremony is open to any adult who wishes to take part.

Prior to the start of the ceremony, the shaman, along with a small group of tribal elders, sets out to locate and collect the peyote buttons. Because of their small size and relative scarcity, finding them can be a long, laborious process. When the first button is found, the shaman sits west of it and prays, "I have found you, now open up, show me where the rest of you are."[12] Sometimes the shaman will eat one or two of the first buttons he finds in hopes of gaining spiritual insight into the location of more of the buttons. The shaman and his group then continue to collect as many buttons as are needed for the ceremony.

When the shaman returns to the village, he and the men and women planning to participate in the ceremony bathe and then dress in ceremonial buckskin clothing. Older men paint their faces in geometric patterns used exclusively for the peyote ceremony. All gather in a round communal tepee or community lodge and sit around the perimeter, leaving the center area open for ritual objects that will be used in the ceremony. These objects include such things as a fire, an

Peyote buttons contain the hallucinogen mescaline, and are used in religious ceremonies by some Native American tribes in the Southwest.

A Lakota Sioux medicine man (left) and Leonard Crow Dog seek spiritual guidance by participating in a peyote ceremony.

altar cloth, drums, the peyote, bowls of water, fruit and meat, a whistle, and cedar incense.

When night falls, the ceremony begins. The shaman starts by standing and announcing the purpose of the ceremony, then offers prayers to the peyote god asking for divine wisdom. He then takes four peyote buttons from a leather bag and passes the bag around the tepee so that everyone may take their buttons. Once everyone has received the raw buttons, they begin eating them. As the tepee fills with incense and the mescaline in the peyote begins to stimulate hallucinations, drums are played and ceremonial songs sung; members wishing to speak about the reason for the ceremony may do so at this time.

During the first part of the ceremony, as they become intoxicated, the participants submit to the effects of the drug, believing that the peyote gives them clear insight for reaching the best decision. The shamans believe that they are able to communicate with the peyote gods while under the influence of the drug. In this regard, they believe the peyote is teaching them. This is when they look to the peyote gods for guidance in helping them make the right decision regarding the purpose for the peyote ceremony.

During the latter part of the ritual, as the effects of the drug begin to wane, the participants turn to thoughtful contemplation and make a conscious effort to understand what the peyote has taught them. More discussion takes place. Occasionally, participants openly weep as they speak, while others begin rhythmic dancing in a trancelike state. As dawn breaks and the effects of the peyote further diminish, water is thrown on the fire. Four morning songs are then sung while the shaman asks each tribal member to give his or her opinion about what decision should be reached.

The last stage of the ceremony is the rendering of the decision by the shaman. Following his pronouncement, the tribal members nod their heads in agreement, and all participants exit the tepee into the morning sun. Members not participating in the ceremony prepare a communal breakfast that they serve to those who took part in the ceremony. Following breakfast, participants pass the remainder of the day with family and friends or sleeping.

The Entheogen Experience

Regardless of the setting or purpose of the ceremony, the effects of mescaline and psilocybin are very similar. About half an hour after ingesting the buttons or mushrooms, the first effects are felt. There are often strong physical effects, including difficulty breathing, accelerated heart rate, muscle tension (especially in the face and neck muscles), and often nausea and vomiting due to the unpleasant taste of the raw substances. Many users blend the entheogens with fruit juice or some type of food to mask the bitterness.

As the psychoactive ingredients take effect, there is a feeling of intoxication and shifting consciousness with minor perceptual changes. Users describe a sense of confidence and feelings of inner tranquillity. As their heart rates accelerate, they experience a heightened awareness of their surroundings and their senses become more acute. Stories of sensory acuity include experiencing more intense colors, sighting apparent halos around objects, and visualizing geometric patterns. Music, which is considered by users an important part of the experience, is described as being more intense than usual and induces in the listeners a soothing trancelike state.

Spatial relationships and time can also become distorted. Familiar objects in a room may appear either smaller or larger than they actually are and may appear closer or farther away than they really are. Some users report seeing objects randomly moving about the room and passing through each other in a ghostlike fashion. Time perception is also affected. Trancelike states that last for several hours are sometimes perceived by participants to have lasted only seconds.

The consumption of hallucinogenic mushrooms can bring on a wide range of effects, including trancelike states, accelerated heartbeat, and nausea.

Halfway through a typical twelve-hour trip, many users experience the onset of what they describe as a quiet phase. During this phase, users describe thoughtful contemplation of themselves, their friends, their families, and their surroundings. Anthropologist Henry Munn, who has lived with and studied several South American and Mexican tribes, documented the experience of one tribal leader who was in a deep peyote trance. As Munn explains, images of nature are a common feature of the hallucinations among indigenous peoples, and most sentences end with the word "says" because the tribal peoples believe the entheogens are talking. Munn recorded the leader's hallucination in a Mexican village:

> Thirteen superior whirlwinds. Thirteen whirlwinds of the atmosphere. Thirteen clowns, says. Thirteen personalities, says. Thirteen white lights, says. Thirteen mountains of points, says. Thirteen old hawks, says. Thirteen white hawks, says. Thirteen personalities, says. Thirteen mountains, says. Thirteen clowns, says. Thirteen peaks, says. Thirteen stars of the morning.[13]

Munn interprets this puzzling hallucination as representing sights common to the tribal leader that are flashing through his mind. The number thirteen, Munn notes, simply represents a large number, not necessarily the literal number thirteen.

For someone living in today's urbanized society, the hallucinations would be different but no less bizarre. For example, in 1953, British writer Aldous Huxley swallowed a dose of mescaline and conversed with a friend who interviewed him about his altered mental state. In his revolutionary book, *The Doors of Perception*, Huxley provided a description of the experience:

> Half an hour after swallowing the drug I became aware of a slow dance of golden lights. A little later there were sumptuous red surfaces swelling and expanding from bright nodes of energy that vibrated with a continuously changing, patterned life. . . . The books, for example, with which my study walls were lined, like the flowers, they glowed, when I looked at them, with brighter colors, a profounder significance. Red books, like rubies; emerald books; books bound in white jade; books of agate; of aquamarine, of yellow topaz; lapis lazuli books whose color was so intense, so intrinsically meaningful, that they seemed to be on the point of leaving the shelves to thrust themselves more insistently on my attention.[14]

Aldous Huxley

British novelist Aldous Huxley's initial psychedelic experience in 1953 was a personal revelation that led to the writing of *The Doors of Perception*, a book which played a significant role in launching the hallucinogenic revolution in America and Europe.

Huxley was born in England to a family famous for a long tradition of scientists. Following his graduation from Oxford University, Huxley began his career as a novelist and essayist. He rose to literary fame for his 1932 novel, *Brave New World*, which depicts a futuristic vision of a totalitarian society devoted to pleasure but suspicious of emotions. In this, his most well-known literary work, Huxley deals with the issue of human freedom in a world where a group called the World Controllers chemically coerced the population into believing that its servitude is pleasurable.

One of the elements of *Brave New World*, which was a foreshadowing of Huxley's later drug experimentation, was the vision of euphoria possible with hallucinogenic drugs. In his novel, there was nothing coercive about drug use. Individuals had the option of using or not using them, but those who chose not to use them were viewed with suspicion by the others.

In 1954, in his book *The Doors of Perception,* Huxley publicly declared himself an advocate of the use of hallucinogenic drugs. For the first time, a large segment of the educated public became aware of the existence of these substances. Not surprisingly, the book created a storm in literary circles. Some hailed it as a major intellectual statement, while others dismissed it as pure nonsense. Few critics realized that the book would have such an enormous impact in years to come.

Huxley openly stated his belief that mind-altering substances, when administered in the right kind of situation, could lead to a mystical experience. He went so far as to predict that a religious revival would come about as the result of further experimentation with hallucinogens. He also stated that drugs would make it possible for large numbers of people to achieve a radical change in how they lived their lives and attain a deeper understanding of the nature of the universe.

Author Aldous Huxley.

Those who use entheogeus such as peote or mushrooms typically report few after-effects. Although most users feel quite tired following the experience, few report experiencing effects such as drowsiness or sickness. What most users do report is a distorted sense of time. Some recovering from their intoxicated state believe they have been in it for weeks, while others believe it lasted only minutes.

Of all the experiences reported by those who use peyote or mushrooms, by far the most common is a sense that they have made direct connection with a deity. Yet fascinating as researchers have found the spiritual component of the use of hallucinogens, they have been even more intrigued with what they saw as the potential some of these drugs seemed to have for explaining the workings of the human mind and for treating mental illness.

Chapter 3

LSD and the Search for Therapeutic Drugs

During the first half of the twentieth century, doctors began to recognize the enormous potential for creating drugs that could cure many common ailments. Pharmaceutical companies expanded their facilities and hired scientists to join in the search for new medicines. One such company was Sandoz, headquartered in Basil, Switzerland, which saw promise in chemicals that are produced by molds called ergot, which are commonly found on grains such as wheat and rye. These compounds, known as ergot alkaloids, were already known for a number of effects, including inducing uterine contractions, stopping bleeding, and relieving migraine headaches.

In 1938, a Sandoz research chemist, Dr. Albert Hofmann, was experimenting with ergot because he believed that the alkaloids it produced might also be an effective medicine for people with breathing and circulation problems. Hofmann knew that the naturally occurring active component of the ergot alkaloid was lysergic acid, and he believed that he might be able to combine it with diethylamide, a synthetic compound, to develop a medicine that would stimulate breathing for asthma sufferers. The combination of these two compounds created lysergic acid diethylamide, which Hofmann named

LSD-25 because it was the twenty-fifth compound developed in a systematic study of combining various chemicals with lysergic acid.

After LSD-25 had been synthesized, it was subjected to pharmacological testing on laboratory animals. One of the secondary effects of the drug that researchers noted was an unforeseen excitement in the movements of the animals. Scientists observed the animals in their cages and noted the nervous twitching and erratic movements. At the time, however, these effects were not considered to be of any interest to the pharmaceutical company; since the new compound turned out not to be effective in treating breathing or circulatory problems, further research on LSD-25 was discontinued.

Hofmann, however, continued to be interested in LSD-25, and in 1943, when he again reviewed the results of pharmacological tests on LSD-25, he decided to investigate the stimulating effect that he had noted the drug had on lab animals. While conducting early experiments, he made an accidental and remarkable discovery. As he was transferring LSD-25 from one glass beaker to another, a small amount of the chemical spilled on his bare hand and as a consequence was absorbed into his body. At this serendipitous moment, Dr. Hofmann discovered the curious properties of LSD, which he later described in a letter to a colleague:

> Last Friday, April 16, 1943, I was forced to interrupt my work in the laboratory in the middle of the afternoon and proceed home, being affected by a remarkable restlessness, combined with a slight dizziness. At home I lay down and sank into a not unpleasant intoxicated-like condition, characterized by an extremely stimulated imagination. In a dreamlike state, with eyes closed (I found the daylight to be unpleasantly glaring), I perceived an uninterrupted stream of fantastic pictures, extraordinary shapes with intense, kaleidoscopic play of colors. After some two hours this condition faded away.[15]

Dr. Hofmann was intrigued by the strange sensations that came over him, although he did not immediately understand what had triggered them. He assumed, however, that it had something to do with the experiments he was conducting in his lab. Hofmann vaguely remembered having spilled the LSD on his hand, and knowing the potency of the ergot compounds, he concluded that his distorted perceptions might be related to the LSD. Hofmann de-

Dr. Albert Hofmann discovered LSD while searching for medicines to treat breathing problems.

cided to conduct a series of experiments on himself with the most minute quantities of LSD that could be expected to produce some effect. He began with what he thought would be a safe dose of 250 micrograms.

Three days after his first contact with LSD, Dr. Hofmann summoned his assistant to observe his behavior after he swallowed the dose. The two men remained in Dr. Hofmann's laboratory, and as evening approached, they rode their bicycles home. Dr. Hofmann reported this historic bicycle ride:

> The altered perceptions were of the same type as before, only much more intense. I had to struggle to speak intelligibly. I asked my laboratory assistant, who was informed of the self-experiment, to escort me home. We went by bicycle, no automobile being available because of wartime restrictions on their use. On the way home, my condition began to assume threatening forms. Everything in my field of vision wavered and was distorted as if seen in a curved mirror. I also had the sensation of being unable to move from the

Dr. Albert Hofmann, when he wrote of his experiments with LSD, did not realize the impact the drug would have.

spot. Nevertheless, my assistant later told me that we had traveled very rapidly. Finally, we arrived at home safe and sound, and I was just barely capable of asking my companion to summon our family doctor and request milk from the neighbors.[16]

As a result of this and many additional experiments, Dr. Hofmann and his colleagues became convinced that they had made an extraordinary discovery, although they did not yet understand the significance that it would have.

The LSD Experience

LSD's major effects, Hofmann and subsequent researchers found, are both emotional and sensory. Initially, there is a slight feeling of anxiety as the user begins to recognize that things are changing from the usual to the unusual. As the effects intensify, emotions may shift rapidly, going from concern, to fear, to euphoria, to meditation, and possibly back again. Sometimes when emotional transitions occur too quickly, the user may seem to experience several different emotions simultaneously.

LSD is best known for its ability to dramatically alter perceptions. Tastes, colors, smells, sounds, and other sensations seem greatly intensified. In some cases, sensory perceptions may blend in a phenomenon known as synesthesia, in which a person seems to hear or feel colors and sees sounds. As with other hallucinogens, the perception of time can also be altered. Some people feel that the hours fly by like minutes, while others feel minutes drag by like hours.

Most users report that they do not find these simple perceptual alterations alarming, but as the LSD trip progresses, the benign altering of the senses often escalates to hallucinations. Cartoon characters

The LSD carried on this square of blotting paper can alter perception of time and cause users to see inanimate objects as having human characteristics.

painted in whimsical colors may float over imaginary forests or fields, or objects such as automobiles feature laughing human faces in place of the headlights and grill.

Although users may find these outlandish images entertaining, hallucinations may also be disturbing. The beat poet Allen Ginsberg described one such hallucination he experienced under the influence of LSD:

> I had the impression that I was an insignificant speck on a giant spider web, and that the spider was slowly coming to get me, and that the spider was God or the Devil—I wasn't sure—but I was the victim. I thought I was trapped in a giant web or network of forces beyond my control that were perhaps experimenting with me or were perhaps from another planet or were

Poet Allen Ginsberg wrote of a disturbing experience with LSD in which he felt he was a helpless speck on a large spider web.

from some super-government or cosmic military or science-fiction Big Brother.[17]

LSD trips may also evolve into intensely personal spiritual experiences. In fact, many writers who explored the effects of LSD explained their principal interest in the drug as being based in a search for spiritual guidance. Psychiatrist W. V. Caldwell defined his LSD-inspired experience this way: "It comprises a religious sense of at-oneness, a resurgence of faith and hope, and a radiant affirmation of the value of life."[18]

As is the case with entheogens, no researcher to date has been able to explain such LSD-induced religious experiences. Psychologist Stanislav Grof, however, observes,

> Some subjects [on LSD] had profound religious and mystical experiences that bore a striking similarity to those described in various sacred texts and in the writings of mystics, saints, religious teachers and prophets of all ages. Despite the fact that many leading scientists, theologians and spiritual teachers have discussed this theme extensively, the controversy about "chemical" versus "spontaneous" mysticism remains unresolved.[19]

Physical and Mental Effects

The effects of LSD typically begin within twenty to sixty minutes following ingestion and may last as long as twelve hours; however, hallucinations generally last about six hours. As with most hallucinogens, the most common physical effects are increased blood pressure and heart rate, dizziness, loss of appetite, dry mouth, sweating, nausea, numbness, and occasionally tremors. In general, these effects disappear once the drug has been eliminated by the body.

Of far greater interest to researchers than the physical effects were the effects on users' mental state. Hofmann and others who experimented with LSD recognized the similarities between its effects and the symptoms of acute mental disorders such as schizophrenia. They both include perceptual distortions and extreme hallucinations. Because of these similarities, Hofmann and his colleagues believed that further research with LSD might provide more clues to understanding and treating a variety of mental disorders.

In addition to providing insight into the nature of mental illness, Hofmann hoped that LSD would prove to be an effective treatment

Nefarious Testing of LSD

Long before most civilians or medical researchers heard that LSD had been dis-covered by Albert Hofmann, the Central Intelligence Agency (CIA) expressed an interest in this new drug. One of the CIA's many concerns when gathering information was determining when spies or informants were lying and when they were telling the truth. During the 1950s, the CIA believed that LSD might be an effective "truth serum." One of the first experiments that the CIA per-formed was secretly slipping a dose of LSD into a drink of a biochemist named Frank Olsen who had agreed to discuss the chemical properties of LSD with the CIA. Two weeks later, Olsen was found dead from a fall from a hotel room that the CIA had rented for him. The newspapers reported his death as a sui-cide, but some who knew Olsen's work for the CIA claimed the CIA agents had pushed him to prevent anyone from learning about the agency's experiment. In 1976, President Gerald Ford publicly apologized to the Olsen family. The president's apology, carried in the *New York Times,* characterized the incident as inexcusable and unforgivable. In addition to the apology, Congress passed a bill in 1976 to pay $750,000 in compensation to Mrs. Olsen and her three children.

Between 1956 and 1967, the CIA and the U.S. Army conducted LSD experi-ments on more than fifteen hundred subjects, many of whom, like Olsen, had the drug slipped into their drinks without their knowledge. The CIA also gave doses of LSD to prisoners in state penitentiaries to see if they would confess their crimes.

In addition to the CIA's interest in LSD as a truth serum, it, along with the army, was also interested in it as a potential chemical weapon. During the 1950s, Dr. Hofmann was repeatedly approached by the army about synthesizing huge quantities that could be used to disorient entire armies on the battlefield.

for disorders like schizophrenia. At the time, the only three treat-ment options available to physicians were antipsychotic drugs, elec-troshock therapy, and a surgical procedure called a prefrontal lobotomy. Each of these therapies had major side effects that made them undesirable, however.

The antipsychotic drugs used during the first half of the twentieth century were powerful sedatives. Since these had to be administered on a regular basis, patients often languish in a drugged state, unable to function outside of their homes or psychiatric hospitals.

The electroshock therapy involved administering a high-voltage shock to the patient's brain, causing convulsions. Patients suffering from severe depression and suicidal thoughts tended to improve temporarily following this therapy, but doctors never fully understood how the convulsions brought on the improvement. This treatment had the drawback of memory loss and brain-tissue scarring. Moreover, patients required repeated treatments since their symptoms always reoccurred.

Scientists looked to LSD as an alternative to conventional treatments for schizophrenia.

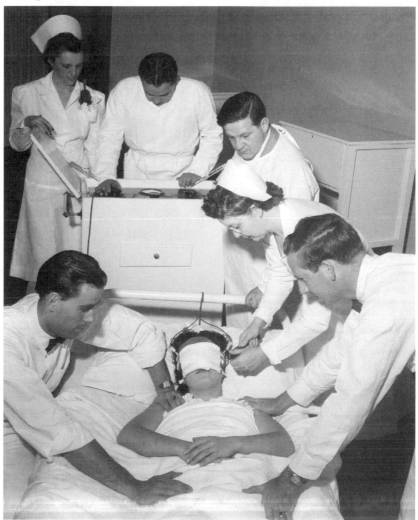

The prefrontal lobotomy was a surgical procedure in which the nerves connecting the prefrontal lobes with the rest of the brain would be severed. The prefrontal lobes are responsible for controlling a person's ability to initiate action, so for patients unable to control themselves, especially those prone to violence, the surgery at least rendered the patients docile and unable to initiate aggression. Unfortunately, the surgery left the patient in a permanent semivegetative state—quiet but unable to function normally.

A prison inmate is prepared for a prefrontal lobotomy, a procedure that was thought to eliminate the part of the brain that induces violence.

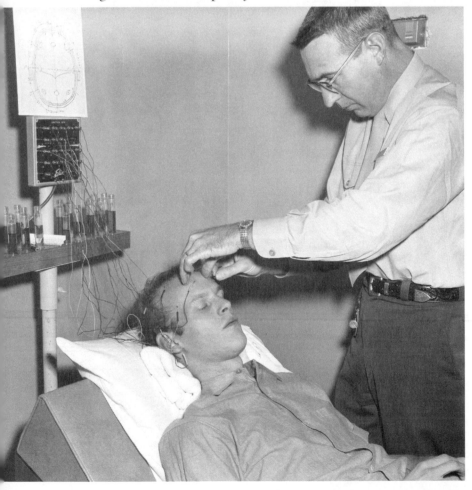

Against this grim background of medical treatments, researchers hoped that LSD could truly help patients with severe mental illnesses. In particular, scientists hoped that LSD might chemically improve the brain's function in patients suffering from various psychoses—particularly schizophrenia.

LSD and Psychotherapy

Since it had repeatedly been observed that extremely small doses of LSD were sufficient to produce changes in perception and behavior that resembled symptoms of schizophrenia, researchers concluded that the brain, under certain circumstances, might produce small quantities of a substance identical or very similar to LSD, and that this could be the explanation for at least some psychoses. If this could be proven, scientists hoped, then schizophrenia and other psychoses could be considered physical, not mental, disorders. The idea that chemicals could alter the brain's chemistry and possibly cause mental illness was revolutionary. Moreover, if this was the case, blocking abnormal mental states by administering medications might be possible. In effect, this could provide a cure for many psychiatric disorders.

In 1953, the German psychiatrist Walter Frederking, in conjunction with several colleagues, was the first to use low doses of LSD in standard therapy sessions to relieve anxiety in patients and to cure various mood disorders such as depression, manic depression, and an assortment of phobias. Frederking and others reported remarkable results from this new therapy, and by the end of the decade, many articles describing LSD therapies claimed various degrees of success. One of the most attractive properties of LSD was that its hallucinogenic effects were not permanent and there appeared to be no other lasting side effects.

In the early 1960s, as LSD research flourished, doctors looked into the possibility that LSD could be a cure for patients with certain mental disorders who were usually considered poor candidates for treatment with psychoanalysis or any other type of psychotherapy. Many individual researchers and therapeutic teams tried treating alcoholics, drug addicts, sociopaths, criminal psychopaths, and subjects with various character disorders with LSD.

One of the first studies on alcoholism focused on administering LSD to alcoholics to see if it could cure their cravings for alcohol. The study found that 53 percent of 135 alcoholics who received a high dose of LSD abstained from alcohol six months after treatment, compared with 33 percent of a low-dose group. Alcoholics receiving conventional therapy had only a 12 percent improvement rate. As research continued, some therapists reported dramatic improvement in patients' symptoms and personalities, sometimes even after a single dose of LSD. Early research also seemed to indicate that the strange and sometimes wrenching effects of LSD amounted to emotional shock therapy with a therapeutic potential similar to electroshocks or other drug therapies.

Other psychiatrists thought that taking LSD themselves might help them better understand their schizophrenic patients and thereby allow them to provide treatment that was more meaningful. Because the hallucinations caused by LSD were nearly identical to those experienced by schizophrenics, researchers also believed that trying the drug could somehow help them learn more about the basic nature of this mysterious mental disorder. Dr. Abram Hoffer, a psychiatrist working in Canada, used LSD and encouraged his colleagues to do the same. Despite such experimentation, Hoffer was never able to correlate his own experience with LSD to any improvements in the therapies he provided to patients.

Even doctors who worked with cancer patients found a possible use for LSD. Although it was never considered as a cure for cancer, LSD was used to ease the suffering of patients with incurable cancer by relieving the anxiety, depression, and acute pain. The treatments seemed to be helpful. In a study of thirty-one cancer patients, 71 percent showed improvement in their emotional outlook after each of several LSD sessions. Researchers also observed that many cancer patients receiving LSD reported that their desire for addictive painkillers, such as morphine, had diminished or even vanished. Researchers believe the success was a result of the brain's ability to disassociate itself from the pain following the initial sensation.

From the late 1940s through the mid-1970s, extensive research and testing were conducted on LSD. During a fifteen-year period

LSD and Chromosome Damage

During the late 1960s and early 1970s, a serious new medical debate was added to the LSD controversy. A number of scientific studies were published indicating that LSD might cause structural changes in the chromosomes, genetic mutations, and disturbances of embryonic development.

The early disturbing research on LSD's effects prompted additional clinical research that contradicted the earlier studies. The new research determined that the first reports of chromosomal damage were the result of studies of illicit LSD users. Some of the subjects did not know the doses of LSD that they had taken, and some later admitted that they had been taking other illicit drugs in addition to LSD. These ambiguities meant that there was no way of knowing whether LSD causes chromosomal damage.

Subsequent studies have failed to find any links between average LSD use and chromosomal damage. Researcher Stanislav Grof, in his book *LSD Psychotherapy Appendix II: The Effects of LSD on Chromosomes, Genetic Mutation, Fetal Development, and Malignancy,* summarized the controversy:

> Two-thirds of the existing in vitro studies have reported some degree of increased chromosomal breakage following exposure to illicit or pure LSD. With one exception, these changes were observed with concentrations of LSD and durations of exposure that far exceeded the dosages commonly used in humans. In none of the studies was there a clear dosage-response relationship. Since similar findings have been reported with many commonly used substances, including artificial sweeteners, aspirin, caffeine, phenothiazine tranquilizers and antibiotics, there is no reason why LSD should be singled out and put in a special category.

beginning in 1950, research on LSD generated more than one thousand scientific papers, several dozen books, and six international scientific conferences. LSD was prescribed to more than forty thousand patients for various reasons.

LSD Beyond the Laboratory

During the 1950s and '60s, LSD research began to move from pharmaceutical laboratories to the private offices of an ever-widening circle of psychiatrists. Within a growing number of settings, psychiatrists were administering LSD to patients in hopes of observing their reactions to the drug and thereby deepening their understanding of its therapeutic effects. Psychiatrists who administered LSD to their patients reported optimistic results. This triggered a variety of therapies involving LSD combined with hypnosis, group sessions, multiday marathon sessions designed to wear down patients' defense mechanisms, toys, and isolation rooms.

At the same time, there were obvious problems with using LSD this way, regardless of the results. Because of the unpredictable nature of the drug, medical professionals consider it unsuitable for therapeutic use. Moreover, LSD advocate Timothy Leary's sideshow-like antics, along with unscientific LSD experimentation by many psychiatrists, turned the government against any kind of research on LSD. In 1974, the National Institute of Mental Health (NIMH) reviewed all LSD research and declared that the drug had no therapeutic value. In the opinion of the NIMH, many of the hundreds of clinical tests conducted since the late 1950s lacked scientific rigor. The NIMH cited the lack of control groups in many studies and the lack of long-term follow-ups of test subjects. When these conclusions were reported to the DEA, that agency ended the use of LSD for research purposes.

Although initial observations on the benefits of LSD were highly optimistic, empirical data developed subsequently proved much less promising. Dr. Robert E. Mogar made the case that LSD may not be all that it appeared to be when he reported,

> Although clinical evidence and testimonial reports indicate that LSD promises to be a valuable tool for both the study and enhancement of cognitive and perceptual functioning, such claims have been neither supported nor refuted by means of controlled studies. [20]

What Mogar was saying, and what some other psychiatrists were suspecting, was that reports about enhanced creativity under the influence of LSD were not supported by objective evidence or scientifically valid research.

Other doctors studied similar claims regarding the use of LSD. Two doctors in Los Angeles, Oscar Janiger and Sidney Cohen, administered LSD to large numbers of patients for the purpose of examining its effects on creativity and personal insight. Janiger sought to explore the relationship between LSD and creativity. He had become convinced that the vividly altered visual perceptions that people experienced under the influence of LSD were the result of a boost in their creative powers. Janiger believed that if he could correlate LSD to creativity, he would be making one of the most profound breakthroughs in history.

To test his theory, Janiger invited numerous painters to his office to work on canvases while under the influence of LSD. After the painters completed several works, a panel of art experts reviewed them to determine whether they could detect an increase in creativity. The experiment yielded no definite answers. After the experts compared notes, there was no consensus one way or the other. When the study ended, Janiger concluded, "Whether or not LSD increased creativity is an open question. Certainly no systematic research to date has been available to help find an answer."[21]

Sidney Cohen went even further, trying to determine whether using LSD could assist people in the intuitive process of applying creative insight into their own lives, personalities, and behavior. Again, the results were ambiguous at best. Cohen concluded that LSD's usefulness might be apparent one session but not the next. Still, he encouraged everyone to try the drug. Cohen's office became a dispensary for LSD; he gave the drug to hundreds of psychologists and psychiatrists, many of whom began boasting of all sorts of psychic revelations, from exploring past lives to conversing with Jesus. LSD experimentation, it seemed, was running out of control.

Much of the problem in trying to demonstrate that LSD enhances creativity is the problem of measuring creativity in the first place. All the studies performed were highly subjective and failed to prove or disprove the claim that LSD had an effect on the creative process. Martin A. Lee and Bruce Shlain, who have written extensively on the history of hallucinogens in their book *Acid Dreams, The Complete Social History of LSD: The CIA, the Sixties, and Beyond*, argue that, although some interesting and highly original works of art have been produced during LSD trips, how the drug affected the creative process cannot be measured. Their belief was shared by many artists, including the "beat poets" of the 1950s and '60s such as Allen Ginsberg and William S. Burroughs. These men, who tried LSD and other hallucinogens, agreed that LSD's creative effects are not measurable in a laboratory setting; however, they continued to believe the effects were very real nonetheless.

Even as the controversy over LSD's effects on creativity continued, others began promoting LSD's use simply as a release from the
boredom of everyday life. Harvard psychologist Timothy Leary
publicly advocated the use of LSD and other hallucinogens for anyone who was interested in experiencing their effects. Leary described
hallucinogens as recreational drugs and spent years urging Americans to have fun with them. He also claimed to teach his followers
how to use drugs safely, but authorities saw him as a destructive influence: At one time, President Richard Nixon labeled Leary the
most dangerous man in America.

Bad Trips

Despite the contentions of Leary and other advocates of LSD use,
the unpredictable nature of the drug's effects means that not all LSD
trips are filled with spiritual awakenings and entertaining hallucinations. According to LSD researchers, "The most common complaint
[about LSD] was an overwhelming state of panic, sometimes involving terrifying hallucinations."[22] This type of panic attack, known
among users as a bad trip, is a temporary condition, but for those
who experience them, the consequences can be serious.

Occasionally, those suffering panic attacks can become aggressive,
and on rare occasions violent. Even if the person experiencing the
bad trip remains calm, confused behavior, fearfulness to the point of
paranoid withdrawals, and even attempted suicide are possible. Bad
trips can last as long as twenty-four hours, although there are undoc-
umented reports of bad trips lasting much longer.

Experts believe that the principal cause of a bad trip is overdose.
Most bad trips occur when people take more than 250 micrograms,
which produces an overwhelming level of serotonin in the brain.

The second cause of a bad trip is environmental. Bad trips often
occur if the drug is taken in unfamiliar or frightening surroundings
in the company of strangers. If people on LSD begin to experience
frightening hallucinations and cannot find a friend or familiar setting
to calm them, the fear can escalate to a panic attack, in which the
sufferer believes that the experience may never end or that he or she
might suffer permanent insanity.

Timothy Leary

The most celebrated and flamboyant proponent of psychedelics from the 1960s was Timothy Leary. Born in 1920, Leary grew up with an interest in psychology and worked professionally as a psychologist, emphasizing the importance of human interaction in therapy. During the 1940s and '50s, Leary tried to revolutionize psychology by proposing radical ideas for the time such as group therapy, which was later recognized as a significant achievement.

When Leary was introduced to psychedelics in 1960, he saw them as a new form of chemical therapy that could possibly change the functioning of the brain in a positive way. While on the faculty of Harvard University, he set out to explore the effects of LSD on the human nervous system. After experimenting with LSD on himself and with friends, he carefully designed and observed laboratory experiments studying the emotional, physical, and social effects on volunteer graduate students. With a large stack of positive results, he believed he was ready to experiment on prison inmates who volunteered to take the drug. However, before these experiments could be concluded, LSD made the headlines as a dangerous new drug and was declared illegal, forcing Leary to abandon his experiments.

Still believing that LSD had great potential, he continued to publicly advertise what he believed to be the beneficial aspects of LSD. As the '60s began to take shape, Leary was cast by the mainstream media, and by himself, as the "LSD Guru," the "High Priest of LSD," and the "Pied Piper of LSD." As the drug gained popularity, he was happy to tour college campuses providing encouragement and instruction manuals for safe usage. He replied to the criticism that LSD was used indiscriminately and for kicks by writing that it should be used indiscriminately and for kicks. As he encouraged people to try LSD, he coined one of the most famous slogans of the '60s: "Turn on, tune in, and drop out," meaning take LSD, experience its spiritual benefits, and drop out of the mainstream culture. In 1966, Leary was arrested on drug charges, and in

1968 Harvard University fired him. He remained in jail until 1976. Subsequently, he moved to California.

In 1996, Leary died of cancer in his Los Angeles home among close friends. According to the Timothy Leary website, Leary's death was videotaped, but the tape has never been publicly broadcast. Surrounded by friends, his last spoken works were "Why not?" which he repeated many times with varying intonations.

Timothy Leary was a psychologist who
influenced the use of LSD.

A bad trip can result from taking LSD while in an unfamiliar location or from taking too much of it at one time.

The third cause relates to the mental health of the user before the drug is ingested. Often, people who are mentally unstable or who have a history of psychiatric problems are at greater risk of having a bad trip. Even among supposedly "normal" individuals, those who are for some reason preoccupied with death or violence are prone to bad trips that focus on death and violent themes.

Occasionally, a bad trip escalates beyond the point where reasonable dialogue can help, and medical attention is necessary. Hospital staff members generally administer sedatives or tranquilizers such as valium or injections of antipsychotic drugs. In almost all circumstances, the person recovers without any long-lasting effects other than the bad memory, although sometimes psychiatric follow-up is required.

Sometimes, bad trips have been known to occur a second time without being induced by a drug. Known as "flashbacks," this phenomenon has recently become the subject of a great deal of debate.

Flashbacks

Those who take hallucinogens—primarily LSD users—occasionally reexperience events or sensations from trips long after the effects of the drug have worn off. Such flashbacks may occur many weeks or even many months after the use of the drug. People who have experienced flashbacks describe them as being as vivid as the initial experiences, although they are aware that they are experiencing a flashback, not a real LSD trip.

Several studies focusing on flashbacks experienced by LSD users indicate that between 25 and 30 percent of those who take LSD have experienced flashbacks at least once. Ten percent of those found them frightening, although none felt that they were actually in danger. The majority reported that the flashbacks did not disrupt their normal routines; a few even said they found the flashbacks pleasurable.

No one knows what causes flashbacks. The first attempts to explain them suggested that minute amounts of LSD had somehow been "trapped" unabsorbed in the user's brain and had dislodged. More recently, however, this theory has been undermined by research that suggests that some flashbacks are triggered by the use of other drugs such as alcohol or marijuana. Still other researchers believe that flashbacks are the result of various forms of stress such as sleep deprivation or a traumatic experience such as the death of a family member or loss of a job.

Some researchers, however, believe that flashbacks may not be caused by LSD at all. They assert that almost everyone experiences flashbacks, which are simply vivid memories of intense emotional experiences. Many people who have never used hallucinogenic drugs report having flashbacks of events such as an automobile accident, the funeral of a close friend or relative, or some violent incident in which they were involved. Soldiers who have experienced combat sometimes report the same fear and panic of battle overcoming them many years after returning home from war. Since LSD trips can also generate intense emotions, these researchers conclude that no differences exist between flashbacks of LSD trips and other memories of significant events. The question of flashbacks and many other unanswered questions associated with LSD use lie at the heart of why LSD use continues to be of concern to the medical profession.

Owsley

The 1960s LSD culture in the San Francisco Bay area produced more than its fair share of cultural icons. One who played a major role was Augustus Owsley Stanley III. Known simply as Owsley to the locals, he was the primary producer of LSD in 1964 before the recreational use of LSD was declared illegal.

During the early '60s when LSD was still legal, few people making it paid careful attention to precisely mixing the chemicals. Many amateur chemists failed to get the mixture right, and the resulting compounds made people very sick or failed to induce hallucinations at all. The other problem was that the doses required to create hallucinogens were so small that precise measurements were hard to perform. As a result, users never knew if the dose was the 200 micrograms advertised or double that amount. Owsley's fame throughout the San Francisco area was based on his precise mixing of the chemicals as well as his accurate dosage.

Owsley hired a chemist from the University of California in nearby Berkeley to make sure his LSD was pure, and he quickly acquired the reputation as a reliable maker of LSD. Many people buying LSD demanded that it be made by Owsley because it was considered reliable. Owsley was the first person to buy a professional press for making pills, and he guaranteed that each pill would contain exactly 250 micrograms of LSD. In keeping with the psychedelic spirit of the times, he manufactured the pills in many different colors and gave each a distinctive name, such as "yellow submarine" and "purple haze."

Owsley charged two dollars a dose, and those prices never changed. Even when LSD was declared an illegal substance, Owsley continued to make LSD. He was not in the business for the money, and everyone respected him for that. Cheryl Pellerin quotes Owsley in her book *Trips: How Hallucinogens Work in Your Brain*: "I never told anybody to go out and take it . . . but . . . I wanted to take it . . . and I didn't want to poison myself. I didn't like Russian Roulette with chemicals."

LSD also continues to be of concern to law enforcement authorities, yet few people are actually prosecuted for possessing the drug. In part, this is because the small quantities in a dose of LSD make it easy to conceal. In part, too, authorities have made a conscious decision to devote their limited resources to eliminating what they see as a much more serious problem: rave drugs.

Chapter 4

Rave Drugs

Just as LSD came to be associated in the public's mind with the culture of the 1960s, two other hallucinogenic drugs, ecstasy and ketamine, have come to be associated with the so-called rave culture of the late twentieth and early twenty-first centuries. These two drugs, which the DEA classifies as hallucinogens, are popular among those who attend impromptu wide-open parties called raves. "Ravers" who take ecstasy and ketamine claim that although these drugs produce perceptual distortions, the effects are mild enough to allow them to dance and converse with friends. Users of ecstasy and ketamine believe that within the rave environment these drugs enhance the experience of dancing to loud music and light shows as well as the enjoyment of being emotionally connected with the large numbers of people who attend raves.

Ecstasy
In particular, ecstasy has a reputation among young people for creating an emotional openness and euphoria that leads to an increased feeling of friendship and empathy for others, relief from everyday stress and worries, and decreased inhibitions. For this reason, psychologists call ecstasy an empathogen, a clinical term for any substance that triggers strong feelings of empathy and emotional closeness to

others, as well as an entactogen, a clinical term for substances that engender an inner sense that all is well with the world.

Acting as an empathogen, ecstasy has the effect of breaking down personal communication barriers such as shyness or insecurity. Users of ecstasy report feeling much more at ease talking to others and that any inhibitions about expressing their feelings toward others, both friends and strangers, seem to disappear. Many people use ecstasy primarily for this effect, reporting that it makes potentially awkward or uncomfortable social situations much more easy to deal with. This effect is so powerful and common that ecstasy is known as a "hug drug." Dan, a raver, recalls experiencing this phenomenon:

A raver swings two glow sticks while under the influence of ecstasy.

We were all trancing pretty heavily, and as I stood with my arms around my two buddies, looking at the ground, I felt that familiar rush of good vibes coming on. All of a sudden, I looked up and found that we were surrounded by 20–30 other people, all hugging in on us, creating a huge circle, the most gigantic hug I have ever been in, and everyone just pouring their love and good vibes.[23]

In addition to this sense of closeness to others, people on ecstasy often describe feelings of being at peace with the world or of experiencing a generalized sense of happiness. Mundane objects may seem to be abnormally beautiful or interesting. People who take ecstasy at raves say that this entactogenic quality enhances the dancing experience. One raver recounts both the empathogenic and entactogenic feelings he experienced:

Users of ecstasy claim the drug makes them feel confident, peaceful, and loving.

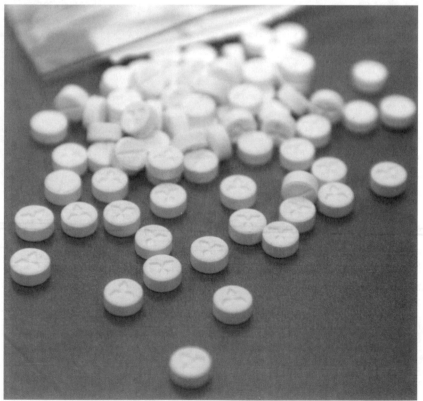

Raves

Raves are cultural phenomena that have sprung up in nearly every urban setting in America and Europe. Hundreds of rave websites promote the parties and provide information about the rave culture, personal experiences, and rave paraphernalia. Initially, raves were known for their remote natural settings at beaches and wooded mountain retreats. They rarely started before midnight, and they frequently kept going until dawn. Now raves occur in nightclubs, empty warehouses, and occasionally sports stadiums capable of accommodating tens of thousands of partygoers. Sometimes they rage non-stop for several days and nights.

In the midst of a rave, partygoers claim that taking ecstasy or ketamine heightens the experience, making it more than just a party with throbbing techno music and lasers and strobe lights. They say it becomes something like a huge family gathering where people feel comfortable with each other without fears of violence.

A wave of warmth overcame me on my way down. For the first time in my life, I knew what empathy felt like. I thought that everyone was my friend, simply due to the fact that those around me (even if I didn't know them) shared and enhanced this feeling just by being around me. The world seemed like a better place. There was no war, no poverty, no pain while I was rolling. I have never felt closer to my friends who were there until then also. We were sharing something that we all knew the others were feeling. We were all in tune with each other's thoughts, feeling, emotions. [24]

Researchers who have studied ecstasy believe that these highly emotional outpourings result from raised levels of serotonin that elevate people's moods. All hallucinogens change levels of serotonin, but ecstasy acts a bit differently. According to Dr. John Morgan, a professor of pharmacology at the City University of New York, other hallucinogens increase levels of serotonin in the synapses by inhibiting its re-uptake in the neurons of the brain. Ecstasy, however, rather than inhibiting re-uptake, actually pulls serotonin out of the neurons' storage locations. This unusual phenomenon results in the synapses of the brain being flooded with a higher concentration of serotonin than they would be when other hallucinogens are used.

Physical Effects of Ecstasy

The physical effects of a standard dose of between 80 and 150 milligrams of ecstasy are subtle and variable. Some users report dryness of mouth, jaw clenching, teeth grinding, mild eye twitching, sweating, or nausea. Others report feelings of profound physical relaxation. At higher doses, the physical effects of ecstasy resemble those of amphetamines: fast or pounding heartbeat, sweating, dizziness, and restlessness.

Researchers do not yet conclusively know if ecstasy causes long-term neurological changes in humans, although animal tests have suggested there is reason for concern. Scientists hold differing views of the implications of using ecstasy, however. Dr. George Ricaurte of the Johns Hopkins Medical Institutions in Baltimore warns, "We now know that brain damage is still present in monkeys seven years after discontinuing the drug [ecstasy]. We don't know just yet if we're dealing with such a long-lasting effect in people." [25] Dr. Charles Grob, an associate professor of psychiatry and pediatrics at the University of California Los Angeles School of Medicine, noted in 1995, "There's no apparent pattern of clinical neural degeneration syndromes reported in millions of people who've taken MDMA [ecstasy] over the last 20 years." [26] However, Richard Glennon, a professor of medical chemistry at the Medical College of Virginia School of Pharmacology, strikes a more cautious note regarding the possible harmful effects of MDMA by stating, "Nobody really has any idea." [27]

Whether it is called ecstasy, E, or XTC, this chemical compound is only available illegally. This was not always the case, however. Ecstasy was first widely used in the mid-1970s as an appetite suppressant, but by the 1980s, psychiatrists also found therapeutic value in the drug's tendency to make people feel happier and boost their self-confidence. Psychiatrists who were treating patients with mild to moderate depression and anxiety reported that their patients said they were increasing their circle of friends and engaging in more group activities.

The success of ecstasy in treating depression prompted more psychiatrists to prescribe the drug for many other ailments. Doctors prescribed ecstasy for complaints ranging from common phobias such as the fear of meeting new people or the fear of flying to nonspecific complaints of unhappiness. Because it seemed to help almost everyone without any noticeable side effects, physicians prescribed it widely. By the early 1980s, with so many doctors writing prescriptions for ecstasy, gradually some of the pills found their way to the illegal street market-place, where its use mushroomed. Ecstasy's illicit use spread so fast that in 1985 the U.S. government banned its prescription use as well as most of its clinical research.

In spite of the drug's illegal status, ecstasy use among Americans continues to expand. According to a 2001 DEA report on ecstasy, "Recent reports estimate that over 2 million tablets are smuggled into the U.S. each week. Current estimates suggest that within the Newark, New York, and Jersey Shore corridor over 750,000 dosage units are being consumed each week."[28] In terms of seizures, the U.S. Customs Service reports that they seized 750,000 tablets of ecstasy in 1998, 3.5 million in 1999, and 9.3 million in 2000.

Despite this phenomenal growth in the use of ecstasy, instances of serious injury or death directly connected to ingesting the drug itself

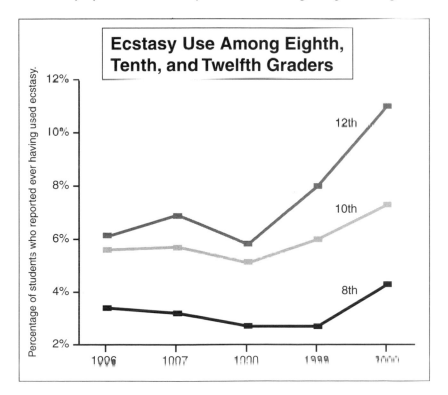

have been relatively rare. According to U.S. coroner's reports filed in 1998, there were nine deaths involving ecstasy. Six of them involved multiple illicit drugs found in the deceaseds' bloodstream, and the three that involved ecstasy alone were all the result of dehydration at all-night raves. Yet growth in the drug's use has been accompanied by a growth in problems. According to the Drug Abuse Warning Network (DAWN), an agency of the federal government that reports on drug use, nationwide hospital emergency room admissions for ecstasy complications rose from 70 in 1993 to 2,850 in 1999.

Loss of Inhibition

Another danger comes from the loss of inhibition that users experience. In the free-wheeling environment of a rave, users often give in to the temptation to engage in unprotected sex. Moreover, users may also find themselves physically unable to resist unwanted sexual advances.

In addition to the risks associated with unprotected sex and the dangers of rape, some enjoying the ecstasy experience have been treated in hospitals for hypothermia—a dangerous drop in body temperature—as a result of removing their clothes and running around outside naked. This phenomenon seems to be unique to ecstasy and is explained by experts as being the result of the sense of well-being induced by the drug. Although there have been no deaths reported from exposure while under the influence of ecstasy, emergency room doctors believe that death from hypothermia in such cases is a possibility.

Deaths associated with ecstasy have occurred from dehydration. Ecstasy causes a rapid loss of body fluids, and when combined with strenuous and long-term dancing in warm environments, that fluid loss becomes extreme. Emergency room doctors who have treated many ecstasy users report that dehydration is one of the major health risks associated with the drug.

Ecstasy and Gang Violence

Whatever the risks associated with using ecstasy might be, society is faced with other problems created by the drug. For example, the growing popularity of ecstasy has sparked violence in America's big cities among gangs who fight for control over the trafficking of the drug.

DanceSafe

In San Francisco, a growing number of partygoers have found themselves in one of the city's hospitals after ingesting unknown drugs at an all-night rave. Not everyone recovers from the effects of contaminated rave drugs.

In 1999, a man named Emmanuel Spirios founded the nonprofit company DanceSafe, in San Francisco in response to the contaminated pill problem. DanceSafe addresses this dilemma with a free pill-testing service at the major rave venues. There are currently twelve DanceSafe chapters across America, with plans to expand to twenty.

When raves are located, volunteers working for DanceSafe set up a table and offer to test anyone's pills to determine if, for example, they are ecstasy. A worker applies a chemical to a sliver of a pill. If it turns a dark purple color immediately, that means that MDMA, the active substance in ecstasy, is present. Another color indicates the presence of some other substance. DanceSafe volunteers have identified thousands of pills that did not turn dark purple. However, a positive test for ecstasy is not a guarantee of safety. Even though the test can positively identify ecstasy, it still cannot measure the dose.

Not everyone is happy with the DanceSafe program. Some believe that providing the pill-testing service merely condones the practice of using illegal drugs and that more ravers will use ecstasy knowing that there is a safe test for it.

Steve Svoboda is head of Chicago's chapter of DanceSafe, an organization that tests pills for contamination.

In part, the problem lies in the fact that ecstasy is highly profitable. Pills that cost no more than fifty cents to manufacture sell for fifty times that amount on the street. Bridget Brennan, a special narcotics prosecutor for New York City, said in an interview, "With drugs, it's always about the money and the dealers are starting to see there is so much money in ecstasy that more people are getting involved, and with that comes more violence."[29]

With money and gang violence come deaths. Gang-related homicides related to ecstasy have occurred in most of America's big cities. Most of these homicides are committed by rival street gangs, but police have reason to believe that organized crime may be behind some of the murders.

In May 2001, New York police arrested a former Gambino crime family hit man, Salvatore Gravano, who later pleaded guilty to running a multimillion-dollar ecstasy ring in Arizona. According to the *New York Times*, "Court documents showed that Mr. Gravano was accused of hatching four homicide plots to consolidate his control of the Arizona drug market, and that his organization was being supplied by Ilan Zarger, a drug dealer based in Brooklyn who had ties to the Israeli mob."[30]

Ketamine

If authorities are becoming increasingly concerned about problems associated with ecstasy, other drugs that are part of the rave scene compete for their attention. Another hallucinogen commonly used at raves is ketamine. Virtually unknown to the public until the 1990s, it nonetheless has experienced a rapid rise in popularity among young people.

Ketamine produces very different effects than ecstasy does. Unlike the friendly social effect of ecstasy, ketamine, commonly referred to as Special-K, K, or Vitamin K, is known at low dosages, between 25 and 100 milligrams, for its quieting and at times calming effects that place users in meditative and introspective moods. The mild sense of inebriation, dreamy thinking, and a sense of the world as being temporary and unimportant is somewhat similar to the effects of LSD, although ketamine's effects are not as long-lasting, wearing off in about an hour.

Salvatore Gravano pleaded guilty to charges of running a large ecstasy ring in Arizona.

At higher doses, however—between 100 and 300 milligrams—ketamine becomes unlike any other hallucinogen. At these doses, ketamine can induce a mild anesthetic state, causing the user to feel tired and dizzy. These effects, combined with hallucinations, frequently cause users to experience a sense of disorientation. One user's recollection of his experience on ketamine is typical:

> What I was feeling at this point: very disoriented, normal reality had just disappeared, physically dizzy and unable to walk without bumping against walls, a bit of paranoia that I was going to die because I had taken way too much . . . mixed with periodic flashes wherein my surroundings would hang motionless and appear really beautiful and I felt totally painless. And sounds were incredibly amplified—I felt like I was in a machine shop or factory. I was pretty confused about what was real. I was too dizzy to stand up, I crashed out on the living room cushions. I started to space on the ceiling, which was flowing. I was cold. I cautioned my friends that they should keep a close eye on me because I might die without them noticing. I couldn't feel if I was breathing (they were watching me the whole time). I could hear them talking but couldn't respond.[31]

Like many other hallucinogens, ketamine affects the user's perception of time. Users report feeling as though time was slowing down to a crawl. Seconds become minutes, minutes become hours, and eventually, as the effect of the drug peaks, some users report that time seems to stop or ceases to have any meaning whatsoever.

Dissociation

Although many of ketamine's effects can be found in other hallucinogens such as LSD, one is unique to the ketamine experience—a sense of dissociation in which the mind seems to leave the body and float in space. Ketamine users often refer to this experience as entering a "K-hole."

Although this experience can be frightening, most users want to experience it and intentionally take a high dose to induce dissociation. The experience of dissociation is, almost by definition, surreal. One user named Paul writes about one of his dissociative experiences:

> In this space I experience myself as a Museum exhibition. I am a life-size statue, with my back to one of the walls, floating about 20 meters from the ground. As I look down, I can see people wandering in and out of the Museum. [32]

Others report that dissociation held some surprises that were not always pleasant:

> Then suddenly, I was back in my body, lying on my bed. "Wow," I thought, "it's over. How abrupt!" I tried to sit up. Suddenly my body was gone again and the room dissolved into the blackness of the void, my reality being quickly pulled out from underneath my feet. . . . This process was actually a little scary, as I had some fear of never making it back to conscious reality, my body lying in a hospital in a vegetative state as my consciousness stayed stuck in a weird, repeating loop. [33]

For some users, dissociation resembles near-death experiences. They report leaving their physical body and sometimes mystically traveling through a tunnel toward "the light." Ketamine can reproduce all aspects of a near-death experience. Many users who have written about their experiences report the conviction of being dead, talking directly to God, seeing heavenly visions, seeing their bodies down below on Earth, entering other realities, and seeing a replay of their life's experiences. Some ketamine users report that they enjoy toying with the idea that they may not return. At the same time, ketamine users have the contradictory experience of knowing that they are not physically near death. Kevin, a regular ketamine user, reports,

I was in a state in which I thought there was a reasonable chance that this time I'd gone too far, and would not come back. I did not feel anxiety about this, just some slight concern (about ending my life with so much still to do). From time to time I would check that my heart was still beating, that I was still breathing and that I could move my hands; each time everything seemed OK, so I was reassured that I had not died. [34]

Physical Effects of Ketamine

As with other hallucinogens, ketamine's psychological effects are unpredictable, being somewhat dependent on the individual user. The physical effects, however, are quite consistent. Ketamine begins to take effect about four to five minutes after injection or ten to fifteen minutes if swallowed in pill form. Initial effects include increased heart rate, elevated blood pressure, difficulty speaking, and loss of coordination. For all its similarities to other hallucinogens, in one way, ketamine is unique: If a large dose is taken, muscle rigidity, respiratory distress, paralysis, cardiac distress, coma, and even death can result.

Near-Death Experiences

Research scientists and psychiatrists are intrigued by claims of near-death experiences (NDEs). They have heard many NDE claims in which people have described crossing over into the next life, seeing a white light, and talking to God. Researchers conduct studies to determine the nature of near-death experiences and what occurs in the brain to create them.

Most researchers believe their studies support the conclusion that NDEs have no spiritual basis. For example, in England, Dr. Karl Jansen has successfully induced NDEs by administering doses of ketamine to volunteers. Jansen's research has focused on the connection between NDEs and elevated levels of serotonin, and his experiments have documented significant increases in serotonin while his volunteers are in the midst of their NDEs.

Michael A. Persinger, a neuroscientist at Laurentian University in Sudbury, Canada, has induced many of the characteristics of an NDE by electrically stimulating the brain's right temporal lobe, the area responsible for perception. In March 1997, an article in *U.S. News & World Report* quoted Persinger as saying that "There's nothing magical about the NDE."

Sherwin Nuland, author of *How We Die*, believes NDEs are caused by opiate-like compounds known as endorphins, which are released by the brain at times of great stress to deaden pain and alleviate fear. Nuland disagrees with those who view NDEs as a temporary bridge to an afterlife: "I think that the mind is just trying to save itself from the horror of unbelievable trauma."

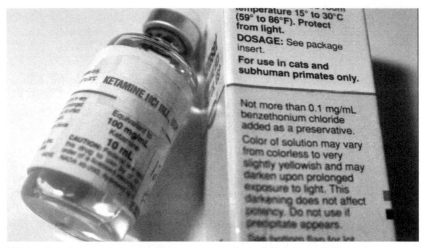

Ketamine has a range of effects varying from fatigue and dizziness to feelings of dissociation.

These dangerous effects of ketamine are rooted in the fact that the drug was originally developed in the 1960s as an anesthetic for use on small animals. At the time, veterinarians were experiencing a high rate of death among animals on which they were operating. For the most part, this was because available anesthetics often caused the animals to stop breathing. As a consequence, researchers began looking for drugs capable of anesthetizing small animals without impairing their respiratory systems. Ketamine was the product of this research, and in 1962 was introduced to veterinarians with great success.

The success of ketamine in cutting death rates among small animals caught the attention of pediatricians, who saw the same need for an anesthetic that would be safe for children. By 1965, ketamine had been approved for use on small children and was hailed by pediatricians as safe and effective.

Thanks to the drug's apparent safety, ketamine's use as an anesthetic continued to expand. During the late stages of the Vietnam War, ketamine became a commonly used anesthetic on the battlefield because it could be administered relatively safely even by nonmedical personnel. This was because an accidental overdose large enough to kill the patient was much less likely to occur than with more potent anesthetics. These wounded soldiers were the first large pool of adults to experience the effects of ketamine, and their stories of hallucinations and mysterious out-of-body experiences caught many medical professionals by surprise.

Word spread of these side effects, and by the 1980s, ketamine's reputation as a hallucinogen and producer of near-death experiences was becoming known throughout Europe as well as America. As a consequence, its use as a recreational drug grew. Recreational users would go to the veterinarian supply companies and purchase the liquid form of ketamine, which they often injected to produce a stronger reaction than snorting the powder form.

Abuse

With increased use of ketamine came increased reports of problems, although, as with other hallucinogens, the numbers are low compared with other drugs. According to DAWN, nationwide hospital emergency room admissions for ketamine complications rose from 19 in 1994 to 396 in 1999. According to U.S. coroner's reports filed in

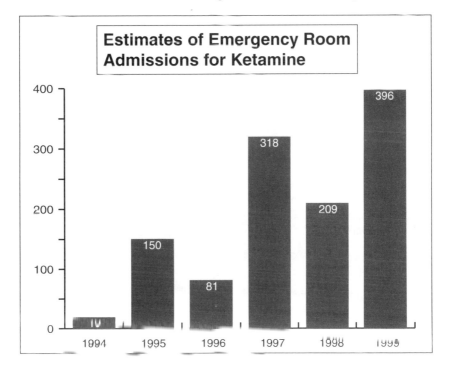

1998, there were ten deaths involving ketamine mixed with other drugs, but none of the statistics indicated how many of the deaths involved ketamine exclusively. Although ketamine's anesthetic properties mean it can be dangerous, those in the medical profession familiar with the effects of ketamine mostly warn users to avoid driving and to remain around sober friends who monitor their behavior and render aid in case of an accident.

One problem with ketamine is that it is one of a growing number of what are known as date rape drugs. Ketamine is odorless and colorless, so it can be added to a drink without being detected. Thus, a victim could unknowingly ingest ketamine, making him or her vulnerable to sexual assault. According to the National Clearinghouse for Alcohol and Drug Information (NCADI), "Because of its anesthetic properties, Ketamine is considered to be one of the 'date rape' drugs, substances that can be slipped into a person's drink to render him or her unconscious." [35]

Furthermore, because of ketamine's numbing properties, which make it an effective anesthetic, and its tendency to induce temporary amnesia, victims frequently have difficulty remembering details about the rape incident. As a result, police and prosecutors have difficulty convicting perpetrators of date rape.

Neurotransmitter Russian Roulette

Perhaps the greatest danger for those who use ketamine is from mixing it with other drugs, which is a potentially deadly matter. National health organizations that study drug illnesses, overdoses, and deaths are universal in their admonition that more Americans die each year as a result of the reckless blending of multiple drugs than from ingesting individual illicit drugs.

According to Dr. Katherine Bronson, a pharmacologist working at the National Institute of Mental Health, people who mix drugs such as ketamine with other substances without the advice of a physician are playing a game of Russian roulette with their neurotransmitters. Hallucinogens affect levels of the neurotransmitter serotonin, as do, for example, most antidepressants commonly prescribed by doctors. When people taking antidepressants add ketamine, for example, the combination can increase the amount of serotonin to the point where it overwhelms the brain's ability to maintain chemical balance.

Mixing drugs that activate different neurotransmitters can also create deadly combinations. Some illicit drug users are in the habit of engaging in what they call "rolling," taking one different drug after another to see what their effects will be. Combining ketamine with a drug such as cocaine, which inhibits the re-uptake of the neurotransmitter dopamine, creates a toxic combination in the synapses that can kill the neurons. According to researcher Dr. William White, "Any combination of drugs with ketamine is extremely dangerous."[36]

Although the dangers of illicit ketamine use have been sounded by many experts, many psychiatrists believe that ketamine still has legitimate uses. In particular, research has focused on helping alcoholics and drug addicts and on curing some forms of depression. Specifically, researchers believe that the near-death experiences can have therapeutic value in helping users acquire renewed interests in self-improvement, spiritual contentment, social recognition, achievement of life goals, and improvement of family and social life. According to Dr. K. L. R. Jansen, "After-effects [of ketamine] can include an enhanced joy in living, reduced fear of death, increased concern for others, reduced levels of anxiety and neurosis, reduced addiction, improved health and a resolution of various symptoms."[37] Yet despite their recognition of ketamine's legitimate applications, the drug continues to concern authorities. The Drug Enforcement Administration keeps track of this and all other hallucinogens and controls access to them.

 **Chapter 5**

Hallucinogens and the Law

The past fifty years have witnessed considerable debate among policy makers over the legal status of hallucinogens, although that debate has yet to reach a clear resolution. Five decades of illicit hallucinogen use by millions of Americans, coupled with legitimate scientific research, have prompted many people to challenge government claims that hallucinogens represent a serious health risk to individuals and to the nation in general. At the heart of this disagreement are the standards that since 1970 have been used to classify certain drugs as illicit while others are listed as legal.

The DEA and Drug Classifications

In 1970, Congress authorized the Food and Drug Administration (FDA) to study all drugs, both licit and illicit, to determine which are potentially dangerous and should be strictly regulated as controlled substances. The Controlled Substances Act, Title II of the Comprehensive Drug Abuse Prevention and Control Act of 1970, is the legal foundation of the government's fight against the abuse of drugs and other substances. This law is a consolidation of numerous laws regulating the manufacture and distribution of narcotics, stimulants, depressants, hallucinogens, anabolic steroids, and certain chemicals that can be used in the illicit production of controlled substances.

If the FDA believes that a specific drug constitutes a potential danger to the public, it places it on the controlled substance list and then notifies the DEA of its decision. The DEA, in turn, determines which of five illicit drug categories, called schedules, is appropriate for the drug. Each schedule specifies different conditions under which a drug can be legally used.

The schedule to which the DEA assigns a drug is determined by whether or not the drug has legitimate medical value and by its potential danger if it is misused by the public. Schedule I is the most re-

The Alcohol Exclusion

The exclusion of alcohol from the DEA's schedule of controlled substances has been widely criticized. Those who support legalizing hallucinogens wonder why drugs they feel are less harmful than alcohol remain on the DEA schedule of controlled substances. The DEA is aware of this inconsistency, but it still opposes the legalization of hallucinogens because it believes alcohol has created many problems in the United States and legalizing drugs would only add to the situation.

Many responsible citizen organizations, however, disagree with the DEA. An independent study of licit and illicit drugs performed by the *Consumer Union Report* concludes, "Until people are willing to enforce alcohol prohibition, ... they are simply wasting their efforts in trying to enforce heroin prohibition, marijuana prohibition, and other drug prohibitions."

According to William Bennett, the "drug czar" for President George H. Bush, in a speech at Harvard University, "We should admit that legalized alcohol,  which is responsible for some 100,000 deaths a year, is hardly a model for drug policy." This number of deaths, however, is considered low by some health agencies. According to the National Institute on Alcohol and Alcohol Abuse, roughly 200,000 deaths a year are caused by alcohol-related diseases, and another 16,000 are due to alcohol related auto accidents.

The DEA's exclusion of alcohol from its list of controlled substances has been widely criticized.

strictive category and Schedule V the least restrictive. Schedule I is reserved for those drugs that have a high potential for abuse, that have no accepted medical value, and that are not considered safe for use even under medical supervision. Because of these criteria, most hallucinogens are Schedule I drugs, as are heroin, cocaine, crack, opium, methamphetamine, and a few others.

The only legal use of a Schedule I drug is for tightly controlled medical and scientific research. The DEA allows legitimate researchers and doctors to apply for licenses to possess Schedule I drugs, but the number of such licenses is extremely small. The DEA has approved about one thousand licenses for physicians and drug companies to handle this class of drugs.

The DEA provides two explanations for why most hallucinogens, which the DEA recognizes are nonaddictive, are grouped with such highly addictive drugs as heroin, cocaine, crack, opium, and methamphetamine. The first reason is that, at the time the Controlled Substances Act was passed and the drug schedules devised, the FDA had already banned their use entirely because no research had yet been conducted to determine the potential danger of hallucinogens. As a result of their unknown potential dangers, when the drug schedules were established in the early 1970s, hallucinogens were added to the Schedule I drugs, and they have remained there ever since.

The second reason hallucinogens are Schedule I drugs, articulated by General Barry McCaffrey, the drug policy adviser, or "drug czar," under President Bill Clinton, is that hallucinogens are "gateway" drugs whose use may lead to experimentation with harder drugs. As gateway drugs, General McCaffrey reasons, if hallucinogens are kept off the streets, there is a reduced likelihood that users will move on to the more dangerous addictive Schedule I drugs.

Four Drug Policy Models

The reasons given by the DEA for grouping hallucinogens in Schedule I along with the so-called hard addictive drugs are rooted in assumptions about drug use, drug users, and their perceived dangers to American society. In fact, much of American drug policy has been driven by a series of specific models, or sets of assumptions, about how illicit drugs operate, affect users, and impact American society. Over the

General Barry McCaffrey, the drug policy adviser in the Clinton administration, feels the use of hallucinogens may lead to experimentation with harder drugs.

past century, four models have evolved, and each one has had an impact on how the nation handles drug offenders.

The first model, called the punitive model, dominated drug policy during the first half of the twentieth century. At its core is the assumption that illicit drugs cause addictive and destructive behavior, which ultimately leads to antisocial and criminal behavior. Those who adhere to this model believe that illicit drugs should remain illegal and that illicit drug users should be punished with incarceration and fines.

During the 1940s and '50s, following psychiatric studies of illicit drug users, a second model called the disease model developed. This model holds that taking illicit drugs leads to uncontrollable addiction, which, like many other diseases, is not the fault of the addict. The disease model further concludes that those who use drugs are victims of those drugs. The assumptions of the disease model are that current drug laws should remain in force, but they recommend counseling and therapy for addicts along with lenient prison sentences.

According to the punitive model of drug policy, illicit drugs should remain illegal and those who use them should be punished with jail and fines.

A third model arose during the 1960s called the social welfare model. Its core assumption is the belief that social and cultural deprivations are the cause of addiction. Factors most often cited include various combinations of poverty, lack of education, unemployment, dysfunctional homes, and pervasive violence. This model advocates the legalization of "soft drugs" such as hallucinogens and infusions of money for education and job training to prevent drug use.

The fourth model, the libertarian model, is the most recent and most extreme. Its core tenet is that the individual is responsible for drug addiction as well as any antisocial or criminal behavior committed while under the influence of drugs. A significant position of those who adhere to the libertarian model is that all drugs should be legal, but the criminal or antisocial behavior they cause should continue to be illegal.

The present model for drug policy in America is a complicated synthesis of these four models. American policy recognizes the need to help addicts with treatment yet also recognizes the need for imprisonment to stop criminal activity. It also expects individuals to accept responsibility for the choices they make—including the wrong ones, which may send them to jail.

At least some experts believe that, with regard to hallucinogens, U.S. drug policy is that all four models that form this synthesis assume that users of all illicit drugs are prone to violence. As a rule, however, most violent drug-related crime in the United States is not committed by people under the influence of hallucinogens. According to a report commissioned by President Richard M. Nixon, *Drug Use in America: Problem in Perspective*, "Except in relatively

Jimmy's Story

Information about drugs and the drug debate can influence public opinion, especially when reported by respected newspapers, magazines, and television news programs. Few citizens are in a position to research news stories to determine their veracity, so stories are more often than not accepted as true and believable.

Sometimes, however, widely published stories about drugs that can influence the debate over drug law reform are false. One such story, "Jimmy's Story," appeared on a front-page feature in the *Washington Post* on Sunday, September 28, 1980. The reporter, Janet Cooke, began a series of articles about an eight-year-old boy named Jimmy growing up in a squalid drug house where drugs such as LSD, marijuana, and heroin were being sold. In subsequent articles, the author described in detail the horrible life of the young boy and the fact that he was an addict.

The response to these articles in the Washington, D.C., community was outrage that an eight-year-old should be subjected to such degrading and harmful circumstances. Jimmy's plight was heralded by organizations opposed to drug legalization as an example of why drugs should never be legalized. Health and school officials began a concerted effort to locate Jimmy and remove him from such an unwholesome environment. When the author of the article was asked to identify Jimmy's home, she refused, citing the need to keep the source's identity confidential. Nonetheless, the search for Jimmy pressed forward unsuccessfully for several months. Meanwhile, Janet Cooke received the most prestigious award a journalist can receive, the Pulitzer Prize, on April 13, 1981.

Just two days later, on April 15, 1981, the front page of the *Washington Post* reported, "The Pulitzer Prize Committee withdrew its feature-writing prize from *Washington Post* reporter Janet Cooke yesterday after she admitted that her award-winning story was a fabrication.

rare instances generally related to drug-induced panic and toxic reactions, users of hallucinogens . . . are not inclined toward as-
saultive criminal behavior." [38] This conclusion is substantiated by
the U.S. Department of Justice, Bureau of Justice Statistics, which
in 1998 reported that of all adults who were under the influence of
drugs when arrested for violent offenses, those under the influence
of hallucinogens ranked lowest behind all other drugs in the report,
which included marijuana, hashish, cocaine, crack, heroin and other
opiates, barbiturates, and stimulants.

Although violence accompanies the rivalries between gangs for
control of the trade in drugs like ecstasy, growing numbers of people
believe that the DEA should separate hallucinogens from addictive
drugs and place them in a different, less restrictive schedule that would
allow for less punitive policies.

Rethinking the Classification of Hallucinogens

One such proponent of reclassifying hallucinogens is Richard B. Karel,
a writer who has researched the problems of drug law enforcement.
He believes that law enforcement agencies should focus on appre-
hending users of drugs associated with violent crime rather than pur-
suing users of hallucinogens. To that end, Karel recommends that
hallucinogens should not be considered as dangerous drugs and believes that "Psychedelics, including the naturally occurring plant drugs
such as psilocybin and peyote, as well as synthetics such as LSD and
MDMA [ecstasy], would be regulated quite differently from all other
drug categories." [39]

The idea that hallucinogens are not as great a threat to the American public as addictive drugs is hardly new. The issue was taken up
in the early 1980s by the Drug Abuse Council, which commented
in the introduction to its report that its board of directors "perceived a pressing need for independent analyses of public drug policies and programs . . . and that the effectiveness of law enforcement
and treatment strategies was often overstated." [40]

The Drug Abuse Council made seven general observations, one of
which focused on the need to recognize that, although hallucinogens
are widely used, they do not present a danger to the public because
they are not frequently abused. The council reported,

> While the use of psychoactive drugs is pervasive, misuse is much less fre-
> quent. A failure to distinguish between the misuse and the use of drugs cre-
> ates the impression that all use is misuse or "drug abuse." . . . The frequent
> depiction of the minority who do misuse drugs, especially illicit ones, as typi-
> cal conveys the mistaken impression that misuse is pervasive if not in-
> evitable.[41]

Thus far, a call for a comprehensive review of drug policy re-
sounds louder than a call for an outright legalization of hallucinogens. To a growing number of Americans, although still a minority,
the prohibition on the use of hallucinogens is viewed as misguided.
Hallucinogens, these critics argue, are nonaddictive and do not belong on the list of illegal drugs along with highly addictive drugs
such as heroin, cocaine, and crack. Furthermore, these critics contend that the health risks for hallucinogen users are insignificant
when compared to a drug like heroin, which, according to the
DAWN reports, annually kills more than four thousand Americans.

*Some critics of America's current drug policy argue that hallucinogens
should not be categorized with highly addictive drugs like cocaine
(pictured), crack, and heroin.*

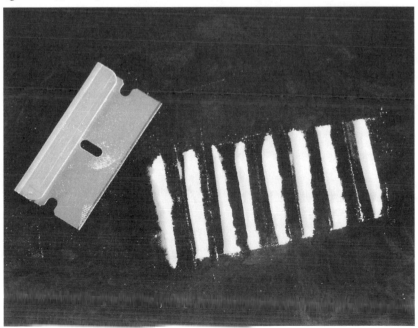

DEA Assertions

In 1974, the DEA published a handbook called "Speaking Out Against Drug Legalization" in which it provided answers and information to DEA agents who "are frequently faced with the need to address many of the positions which are advocated by those calling for the legalization of drugs. . . . Legalization, however, is not an alternative, but rather a surrender that will further reduce our quality of life."

In addition to many tips and pieces of information to use when debating against the legalization of illicit drugs, the DEA listed the following ten assertions it believes to be factually true:

Assertion 1:   Crime, violence and drug use go hand in hand.

Assertion 2:   We have made significant progress in reducing drug use in this country. Now is not the time to abandon our efforts.

Assertion 3:   Legalization of drugs will lead to increased use and increased addiction levels.

Assertion 4:   Any revenues generated by taxing legalized drugs would quickly evaporate in light of the increased social costs associated with legalizing drugs.

Assertion 5:   There are no compelling medical reasons to prescribe marijuana or heroin to sick people.

Assertion 6:   Legalization and decriminalization of drugs have been a dismal failure in other nations.

Assertion 7:   Alcohol has caused significant health, social and crime problems in this country, and legalized drugs would only make the situation worse.

Assertion 8:   Drug control spending is a minor portion of the U.S. budget, and compared to the costs of drug abuse, spending is minuscule.

Assertion 9:   Drug prohibition is working.

Assertion 10:   Drug legalization would have an adverse effect on low income communities.

Despite the growing demand to reconsider hallucinogen laws, the DEA is adamantly opposed to any change in policy regarding legalization of hallucinogens. In its publication titled Speaking Out Against Drug Legalization, the DEA states, "Legalization, however, is not an alternative, but rather a surrender that will further reduce our quality of life."[42] DEA leadership, supported by the president and many congressional leaders, believe that the current laws are fair, effective, and necessary for the good of the nation. Calls for any change in drug policies, the DEA contends, would be a serious mistake. Directors of the DEA believe the prohibition on hallucinogens is a successful and necessary policy. Legalization of these drugs, they contend, would lead to increased use.

Peyote, American Indians, and the Law

One hallucinogen already has the unique status of being legally used under one specific circumstance: peyote. The Justice Department has made this one exception to accommodate a claim that peyote is a necessary part of a religious ritual.

Peyote has been a part of the religious ceremonies for several American Indian tribes for many generations. During the 1930s, when states passed laws prohibiting the use of peyote, members of the Native American Church, who had been using peyote in their religious ceremonies, protested the prohibitions. They fought the

The use of peyote as part of religious rituals is legal for members of the Native American Church.

peyote prohibition in the courts, citing their rights to religious freedom and religious practices as guaranteed under the First and Four-
teenth Amendments to the U.S. Constitution.

Attorneys arguing before the Albuquerque District Court on be-
half of the Native American Church pointed out that, for hundreds of
years, peyote had been viewed as a natural gift of God to humankind,
and especially to natives of the land where it grows. They argued that
no government has a right to tamper with traditional religious rituals.

In 1960, the Albuquerque District Court ruled in favor of the Native American Church, allowing them to legally use peyote as part of
their religious ceremonies. Peyote remains on the DEA's list of
Schedule I drugs; however, this prohibition does not apply to bona
fide religious ceremonies of the Native American Church. Controls
over peyote use are still closely regulated, and any person who pre-
pares peyote or distributes peyote to the Native American Church is
required to obtain annual registration from the DEA and to comply
with all other requirements of the law.

Problems of Law Enforcement

The DEA adamantly opposes any further exceptions to the ban on
Schedule I drugs. Yet this position presents most law enforcement
agencies with a problem. Attempting to enforce all drug laws has become a near-impossible task for federal and local law enforcement
agencies. Limited budgets and manpower exhaust the ability of nearly
all police departments to keep up with the millions of Americans using
a wide variety of illicit drugs.

Yet police agencies prefer not to be given the added job of deciding
whether or not a particular law or regulation should be enforced. A
spokesperson for the International Association of Chiefs of Police
(IACP) stated that the policy of that group's members is to enforce all
drug laws, including nonviolent hallucinogen use, without regard for
their perceived seriousness. This has been a long-standing position because the job of law enforcement officers is to enforce drug laws, not
pass judgment on whether the laws merit enforcement or not.

In 1996, however, the New York County Lawyers' Association
(NYCLA) called for changes in drug laws to relieve law enforcement
officers, such as members of the IACP, from the need to use valuable

Urban Legends and Hallucinogens

Many urban myths–false stories that are repeated as if they are true–have focused on hallucinogens, especially LSD. Often, these legends originate with people who believe that terrifying stories will deter illicit drug use.

One of the earliest urban myths that circulated in hundreds of newspapers was a story about a group of LSD users who began staring at the sun. The people portrayed in the story were allegedly so high that they failed to realize that they were blinding themselves until someone found them and pointed out to them that they had destroyed their retinas.

Another urban legend, circulated primarily on the Internet, warned people that the push buttons on public pay phones in some cities had been contaminated with LSD, and touching them would cause the victim to absorb a dangerously high dose of LSD through their finger tips. After a great deal of research by several groups, including the federal government's Centers for Disease Control and Prevention, this warning was determined to be a hoax. Yet it continues to surface from time to time.

Of all the LSD urban legends, the oldest and most well known is that of the blue-star tattoo. The story was first circulated by a church in 1992 that warned parents of LSD placed on children's stick-on tattoos that look like blue stars. The church flyer went on to say that this was a strategy used by drug pushers to hook children on LSD. The blue-star tattoo story was quickly picked up by dozens of major newspapers that failed to research it. Eventually, most of the newspapers debunked this myth.

Yet some contend that such urban myths, though untrue, still serve a purpose. As David Emery points out on his website Urban Legends and Folklore, "Are children really in danger of getting dosed with LSD through drug-laced tattoos? No. Are they endangered by the careless drug use of the adults around them? Clearly, they can be. This is another example of how a false story can paint a true picture of the things we most fear."

resources enforcing laws against hallucinogen use, which the NYCLA said is creating "a clogged criminal justice system unable to focus on society's larger crime problems. Courts jammed with drug cases inevitably results in insufficient resources available to properly attend to these [violent drug crimes] and other more serious crimes appearing on overburdened court dockets."[43]

In fact, the DEA admits that confiscating hallucinogens such as LSD is such a low priority, it has virtually stopped attempting to do so. A report in one DEA publication summarizes the agency's position: "Six clandestine LSD synthesis laboratories have been confiscated by

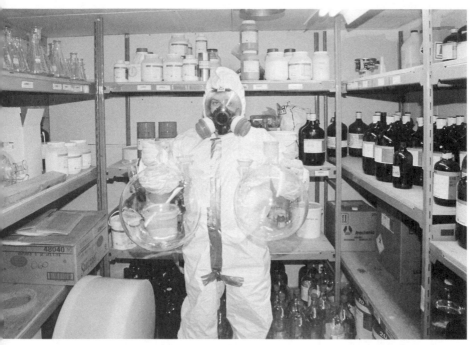

An undercover drug officer removes two flasks from a lab where drugs had been illegally manufactured.

[the] DEA since 1981; however, there have been no seizures since 1987. This is due primarily to . . . the crack epidemic that began during the mid-1980's and continues into the present."[44] The report by the DEA does not mean that it no longer enforces laws governing the use of hallucinogens, but it does indicate that its hands are tied by more serious, violent drug-related crimes in need of its limited resources.

Government Responsibilities vs. Individual Rights

Many people believe that the most fundamental issue involving hallucinogens and the law is the question of whether the government has the right in the first place to determine that hallucinogens cannot be legally purchased by the citizenry. This question represents a clash between the responsibility of the government to protect citizens from danger and the rights of individuals to decide for themselves how they conduct their lives.

For many Americans, however, controlling drugs and their use is sound public policy. Three drug researchers, Kenneth Jones, Louis Shainberg, and Curtis Byer, who study hallucinogens as well as other illicit drugs, assert,

> [Drug laws] have been enacted to protect society. Legal controls such as quarantines, isolation, and penalties have always been necessary to stop the spread of various diseases and illnesses. Since the best evidence supports the view that compulsive drug abuse is an indication of an emotional illness in an individual, society is justified in insisting on some type of regulation on the manufacture, distribution, and use of drugs. Such regulation can be viewed as a part of preventative medicine.[45]

Although the views of Jones, Shainberg, and Byer are supported by many people, many opponents of the current policy governing hallucinogens challenge the idea that users of hallucinogens are compulsive drug abusers.

Besides the issue of determining which drugs are dangerous, many people believe that adults have the right to determine what substances they consume, regardless of whether the government thinks they are dangerous. A study released by the New York County Lawyers' Association regarding personal drug choices concluded, "In recognition of inherent rights to privacy and personal autonomy, reevaluate whether, and to what degree, government intervention is appropriate and justifiable with respect to casual use of drugs by its citizens."[46]

The conflicting interests of the government's responsibility to protect its citizens and the individual's right to make choices are often difficult to reconcile. Very often, defining what constitutes a danger is open to considerable disagreement among reasonable people. In any case, the Drug Abuse Council recognizes that to try to eliminate the use of hallucinogens is perhaps unrealistic: "Some psychoactive drugs are almost always readily available to enable people to achieve what they wish or need for alteration of mood or mind."[47]

The search for altered perceptions can take many different paths, only one of which is drug-induced. The use of hallucinogens began with the earliest civilizations and continues to the present. Whether for spiritual, medical, or recreational use, hallucinogens, far from falling into disfavor and disappearing from the human record, continue to be sought out and used in virtually all cultures regardless of their legal status.

Regardless of how many people use hallucinogens or why they do so, there remains an uneasiness that surrounds the unpredictability of their effects. Drug awareness groups such as the National Clearing-house for Alcohol and Drug Information and the National Institute on Drug Abuse have raised the question whether other methods could be found to alter moods and to achieve altered states of consciousness that do not involve drugs.

Dr. Vincent Nowlis, a psychologist at the University of Rochester, along with several colleagues, made the observation that throughout history people have found many ways to change moods and alter consciousness without using drugs. Most notably, he points to physical and spiritual experiences, diet, rest, recreation, travel, and the simple pleasures of music, theater, and sports.

Ecstasy (shown here) and other hallucinogens continue to be sought out and used regardless of their legal status.

Yet hallucinogens continue to be a part of American drug culture. Despite their continued use by significant numbers of Americans, the legal status of hallucinogens is unlikely to change soon. To the satisfaction of those opposing their legalization, hallucinogens are likely to remain on the DEA's Schedule I list of controlled substances for the foreseeable future. But, to the satisfaction of those who want to use them, hallucinogens are likely to remain available. Whether the use of hallucinogens will change and whether the laws governing hallucinogen use will or should be modified are questions that will continue to be part of the public debate over America's drug policy.

Blank page

Notes

Chapter 1: A Strange Class of Drugs

1. Quoted in the Vaults of Erowid, "Enveloped by All of Nature." www.erowid.org/experiences/exp.php3?ID=1978.
2. Quoted in the Vaults of Erowid, "Impossible to Understand Reality." www.erowid.org/experiences/exp.cgi?ID=1979.
3. Quoted in the Vaults of Erowid, "Enveloped by All of Nature."
4. Solomon Snyder, *Drugs and the Brain*. New York: Scientific American Books, 1986, p. 207.
5. National Institute on Drug Abuse, "LSD." www.nida.nih.gov/Infofax/lsd.html.
6. Martin H. Keeler and Clifford B. Reifler, "Suicide During an LSD Reaction," *American Journal of Psychiatry*, January 7, 1967, p. 885.

Chapter 2: Hallucinogens and Spiritual Rituals

7. Quoted in *Heffter Review of Psychedelic Research* "Antiquity of the Use of New World Hallucinogens." www.heffter.org.
8. Quoted in the Lycaeum, "Prehistoric Psychoactive Mushroom Artifacts." www.lycaeum.org/drugs.old/plants/mushrooms/tassili2.html.
9. Henry Munn, *Hallucinogens and Shamanism*. Ed. Michael J. Harner. Oxford, England: Oxford University Press, 1973, p. 47.
10. Quoted in Munn, *Hallucinogens and Shamanism*, p. 51.
11. Quoted in Munn, *Hallucinogens and Shamanism*, p. 61.
12. Quoted in Weston La Barre, *The Peyote Cult*. Norman: University of Oklahoma Press, 1989, p. 43.
13. Quoted in Munn, *Hallucinogens and Shamanism*, p. 43.
14. Aldous Huxley, *The Doors of Perception and Heaven and Hell*. New York: Harper Perennial, 1990, p. 39.

Chapter 3: LSD and the Search for Therapeutic Drugs

15. Albert Hofmann, *LSD, My Problem Child*. Trans. Jonathan Ott. New York: McGraw-Hill, 1980, p. 28.
16. Hofmann, *LSD, My Problem Child*, p. 35.
17. Quoted in Martin A. Lee and Bruce Shlain, *Acid Dreams, the Complete Social History of LSD: The CIA, the Sixties, and Beyond*. New York: Grove Press, 1986, p. 73.
18. Quoted in Richard Leiby, "The Magical Mystery Cure, Richard Yensen, Psychologist Experimenting with LSD," *Esquire*, September 1, 1997, p. 101.
19. Stanislav Grof, *LSD Psychotherapy*, Alameda, CA: Hunter House, 1980, p. 14.
20. Robert E. Mogar, "Current Status and Future Trends in Psychedelic (LSD) Research," *Journal of Human Psychology*, vol. 2, 1965, p. 161.
21. Quoted in Cheryl Pellerin, *Trips: How Hallucinogens Work in Your Brain*. New York: Seven Stories Press, 1998, p. 63.
22. R. G. Smart and D. Jones, "Illicit LSD Users: Their Personality Characteristics and Psychopathology," *Journal of Abnormal Psychology*, June 1970, p. 288.

Chapter 4: Rave Drugs

23. Council on Spiritual Practices, "The Hug." www.csp.org.
24. Ecstasy.org, "Empathy Through Ecstasy." www.ecstasy.org.
25. Quoted in Drug Enforcement Administration, "Ecstasy Damages the Brain and Impairs Memory in Humans." www.usdoj.gov/dea/concern/mdma/ecstasy020700.htm.
26. Quoted in Pellerin, *Trips*, pp. 151–52.
27. Quoted in Pellerin, *Trips*, p. 153.
28. Drug Enforcement Administration, "3, 4 Methylenedioxymethamphetamine (MDMA, XTC, X, Ecstasy, Adam)." www.usdoj.gov/dea/concern/mdma/mdma020700.htm.
29. Quoted in *New York Times*, "Violence Rises as Club Drug Spreads Out into the Streets," June 24, 2001, p.1.
30. *New York Times*, "Violence Rises as Club Drug Spreads Out into the Streets," p. 1.

31. Quoted in the Vaults of Erowid, "Pure Light." www.erowid.org/experiences/exp.php3?ID=1962.
32. Quoted in the Vaults of Erowid, "Ketamine Info." www.erowid.org/chemicals/ketamine/ketamine_info1.shtml.
33. Quoted in the Vaults of Erowid, "Peeking Behind the Curtain." www.erowid.org/experiences/exp.php3?ID=1977.
34. Quoted in Peter Meyer, "Report on a Ketamine Experience." http://serendipity.magnet.ch/dmt/ket89.html.
35. National Clearinghouse for Alcohol and Drug Information, *Prevention Works! Club Drugs: Ketamine*, September 1, 2000, p. 8.
36. William White, "This Is Your Brain on Dissociatives: The Bad News Is Finally In," Lycaeum, http://leda.lycaeum.org/Documents/This_Is_Your_Brain_On_Dissociatives:_The_Bad_News_is_Finally_In.9299.shtml.
37. K. L. R. Jansen, "Ketamine and Quantum Psychiatry," *Asylum*, vol. 11, no. 3, 1999, p. 19.

Chapter 5: Hallucinogens and the Law

38. National Commission on Marijuana and Drug Abuse, commissioned by President Richard M. Nixon, *Drug Use in America: Problem in Perspective*, March 1972, Schaffer Library of Drug Policy. www.druglibrary.org/schaffer/Library/studies/du-apip/pip3.htm.
39. Richard B. Karel, *The Drug Legalization Debate: Studies in Crime, Law, and Justice*. Vol. 7, London: Sage, 1991, p. 161.
40. Drug Abuse Council, "The Facts About Drug Abuse," 1980, Schaffer Library of Drug Policy. www.druglibrary.org/schaffer/library/studies/fada/fadafin.htm.
41. Drug Abuse Council, "The Facts About Drug Abuse."
42. Drug Enforcement Administration, "Speaking Out Against Drug Legalization," www.usdoj.gov/dea/demand/druglegal/intro.htm.
43. New York County Lawyers' Association, "Report and Recommendations of the Drug Policy Task Force," October 1996, Schaffer Library of Drug Policy. www.druglibrary.org/schaffer/

library/studies/nycla/nycla.htm.
44. Drug Enforcement Administration, "LSD in the United States." www.usdoj.gov/dea/pubs/lsd/toc.htm.
45. Kenneth L. Jones, Louis W. Shainberg, and Curtis O. Byer, *Drugs and Alcohol.* New York: Harper & Row, 1969, pp. 69 70.
46. New York County Lawyers' Association, "Report and Recommendations of the Drug Policy Task Force."

Organizations to Contact

Drug Enforcement Administration (DEA)
2401 Jefferson Davis Hwy.
Alexandria, VA 22301
(202) 307-8846
website: www.usdoj.gov/dea/index.htm

The DEA website is maintained by the Department of Justice to provide the public with access to general information about the status of illegal drug use in the United States.

National Clearinghouse for Alcohol and Drug Information (NCADI)
11426-28 Rockville Pike, Suite 200
Rockville, MD 20852
(800) 729-6686
website: www.health.org/Index.htm

The NCADI is the information service of the Center for Substance Abuse Prevention in the U.S. Department of Health and Human Services. NCADI is the world's largest resource for current information and materials concerning substance abuse.

National Institute on Drug Abuse (NIDA)
6001 Executive Blvd., Room 5213
Bethesda, MD 20892-9651
(301) 443-1124
website: http://165.112.78.61/NIDAHome.html

The NIDA provides the latest information on drug abuse in America. Its information focuses on research as well as statistics on drug use and focuses on warning the public of the risks involved with drug use.

Substance Abuse and Mental Health Services Administration (SAMHSA)
5600 Fishers Lne.
Rockville, MD 20857
(301) 443-8956
website: www.samhsa.gov

SAMHSA is the federal agency charged with improving the quality and availability of prevention, treatment, and rehabilitative services in order to reduce illness, death, disability, and cost to society resulting from substance abuse and mental illnesses.

For Further Reading

Peter Matthiessen, *Snow Leopard*. New York: Viking Press, 1978. This is a beautifully written adventure book about the search for the rare snow leopard in the Himalayan Mountains of Tibet. Written in journal format, the book also brings to life the author's experiences with hallucinogens, his introspective journey while describing the Tibetan culture, and the history of Buddhism.

Leonard Uhr and Elizabeth Uhr, *Readings in Social Psychology Today*. Del Mar, CA: CRM Books, 1970. This is an anthology of many studies in social psychology, many of which apply to hallucinogen use and potential health problems.

R. G. Wasson, *Soma: Divine Mushroom of Immortality*. New York: Harcourt Brace Jovanovich, 1971. This work is considered a classic entheogen compendium covering all facets of the spiritual uses of hallucinogens, particularly mushrooms. It discusses the similarities and differences between mushrooms in many countries and includes maps and illustrations.

Tom Wolfe, *The Electric Kool-Aid Acid Test*. New York: Bantam, 1968. This novel is a 1960s pop-culture literary icon about Ken Kesey and his band of Merry Pranksters. It describes the relatively carefree days of LSD use in California among the hippies and the politics of the times. Although a fictionalized account of the times, it remains a best-seller because of its accurate depiction.

Works
Consulted

Books

Peter Furst, *Hallucinogens and Culture*. San Francisco: Chandler & Sharp, 1976. This book provides a comprehensive history of hallucinogenic use among early tribes and civilizations. Furst deals with the chemistry of hallucinogenic plants as well as the mysticism that surrounds their cultural uses.

Erich Goode, *Drugs in American Society*. New York: Alfred A. Knopf, 1972. This is an anthology of several psychologists and sociologists that presents a variety of views on drugs and the laws that govern them in America.

Stanislav Grof, *LSD Psychotherapy*. Alameda, CA: Hunter House, 1980. This work is a comprehensive history of the use of LSD in psychotherapy. The author discusses the many modalities of LSD in therapeutic settings and provides excellent support for all conclusions drawn regarding the use and abuse of LSD by the medical profession.

———, *LSD Psychotherapy Appendix II: The Effects of LSD on Chromosomes, Genetic Mutation, Fetal Development, and Malignancy*. Alameda, CA: Hunter House, 1994. This is a highly academic work reviewing all medical and clinical research on the possible effects of LSD on human chromosomes. It is written for the research community.

Albert Hofmann, *LSD, My Problem Child*. Trans. Jonathan Ott. New York: McGraw-Hill, 1980. The Swiss chemist Albert Hofmann his involvement with LSD, from his early experiments through his later work. Hofmann also discusses the many dilemmas he faced in the course of his work with LSD.

Aldous Huxley, *The Doors of Perception* and *Heaven and Hell*. New York: Harper Perennial, 1990. This volume contains two classic works by Huxley. *The Doors of Perception* documents Huxley's experience with mescaline.

Kenneth L. Jones, Louis W. Shainberg, and Curtis O. Byer, *Drugs and Alcohol*. New York: Harper & Row, 1969. This book makes the argument that laws are necessary to control the spread of drug and alcohol use because of the inherent danger that these drugs can cause.

Richard B. Karel, *The Drug Legalization Debate: Studies in Crime, Law, and Justice*. Vol. 7, London: Sage, 1991. This book discusses many of the issues surrounding the legalization of illicit drugs in America.

Weston La Barre, *The Peyote Cult*. Norman: The University of Oklahoma Press, 1989. This book provides a relatively detailed explanation of the origins of the peyote cult as well as many examples of different ceremonies, mostly in the Southwest United States.

Martin A. Lee and Bruce Shlain, *Acid Dreams, the Complete Social History of LSD: The CIA, the Sixties, and Beyond*. New York: Grove Press, 1986. This work tells a full and colorful cultural story of LSD from the Summer of Love in San Francisco until the time it was published. In addition to discussing all of the major people associated with LSD, clinical and casual experiments, and the effects of LSD, the authors also tell the story of the CIA's involvement with the drug.

Henry Munn, *Hallucinogens and Shamanism*. Ed. Michael J. Harner. Oxford, England: Oxford University Press, 1973. This book is a collection of experiences recorded by modern anthropologists living with and studying primitive tribes in Mexico and South America. Each anthropologist reports on different tribes and the cultural connections between the tribes, their shamans, and hallucinogens.

Ray Oakley and Charles Ksir, *Drugs, Society, and Human Behavior*. New York: McGraw-Hill, 1999. This is a college textbook that presents a broad spectrum of research examining drugs from all perspectives, including behavioral, pharmacological, historical, social, legal, and clinical. All families of drugs are covered.

Cheryl Pellerin, *Trips: How Hallucinogens Work in Your Brain*. New York: Seven Stories Press, 1998. This is an excellent yet slightly irreverent look at hallucinogens and how they affect the brain. The book contains ample references to illicit drug chemistry and is heavily laced with expert testimony and delightful cartoons illustrating chapter themes. It also has an excellent bibliography, including dozens of websites.

Nicholas Saunders, Anja Saunders, and Michelle Pauli, *In Search of the Ultimate High.* London: Random House, 2000. This study of entheogens and their spiritual importance provides a history of hallucinogens used in religious ceremonies. The book covers the use of LSD, mushrooms, peyote, and dozens of other psychoactive drugs used in spiritual quests as well as how different cultures use them.

Solomon Snyder, *Drugs and the Brain.* New York: Scientific American Books, 1986. This work focuses on the pharmacology of drugs and how they interact with the brain. Although it provides detailed information, it is written for the intelligent yet ignorant reader.

D. M. Turner, *The Essential Psychedelic Guide.* San Francisco: Panther Press, 1994. This book provides detailed descriptions of the chemistry, health issues, and effects of all major psychedelic drugs.

R. Gordon Wasson, Albert Hofmann, and Carl Ruck, *The Road to Eleusis: Unveiling the Secret of the Mysteries.* New York: Harcourt Brace Jovanovich, 1978. This book attempts to answer the question of what substance was consumed during the annual ritual of the Eleusinian Mysteries in Greece.

Periodicals

K. L. R. Jansen, "Ketamine and Quantum Psychiatry," *Asylum,* vol. 11, no. 3, 1999.

Martin H. Keeler and Clifford B. Reifler, "Suicide During an LSD Reaction," *American Journal of Psychiatry,* January 7, 1967.

Brendan I. Koerner and Joshua Rich, "Is There Life After Death?" *U.S. News & World Report,* March 31, 1997.

Paula Kurtzweil, "Medical Possibilities for Psychedelic Drugs," *Federal Drug Administration Consumer,* September 1, 1995.

Richard Leiby, "The Magical Mystery Cure, Richard Yensen, Psychologist Experimenting with LSD," *Esquire,* September 1, 1997.

Louise Milligan, "Serotonin: The Secret Ingredient," *Australian,* April 21, 2001.

Robert E. Mogar, "Current Status and Future Trends in Psychedelic (LSD) Research," *Journal of Human Psychology*, vol. 2, 1965.

National Clearinghouse for Alcohol and Drug Information, *Prevention Works! Club Drugs: Ketamine*, September 1, 2000.

New York Times, "Violence Rises as Club Drug Spreads Out into the Streets," June 24, 2001.

R. G. Smart and D. Jones, "Illicit LSD Users: Their Personality Characteristics and Psychopathology," *Journal of Abnormal Psychology*, June 1970.

Websites

Council on Spiritual Practices (www.csp.org). The Council on Spiritual Practices is a collection of spiritual guides, experts in the behavioral and biomedical sciences, and scholars of religion who make different types of spiritual experiences available to the public. This website provides interviews with a large cross-section of people who have had spiritual experiences.

Drug Enforcement Administration (www.usdoj.gov/dea/directory. htm). The Drug Enforcement Administration (DEA) website is maintained by the Department of Justice to provide the public with access to general information about the status of illegal drug use in the United States. The site includes statistics, discussions, publications, and other topics affecting the DEA.

Ecstasy.org (www.ecstasy.org). Ecstasy.org is a website dedicated to disseminating information about ecstasy, including medical research, articles, books, personal experiences, and questions and answers.

Heffter Research Institute (www.heffter.org). This website provides a database of technical articles about research on hallucinogens.

Lycaeum (www.lycaeum.org/live/). The Lycaeum is a nonprofit drug-information archive that promotes awareness about the effects, chemistry, and history of various hallucinogens. The majority of its information focuses on peyote and mushrooms.

National Institute on Drug Abuse (www.nida.nih.gov). NIDA's mission is to lead the nation in bringing the power of science to bear on drug abuse and addiction. NIDA conducts research on drugs and disseminates its results to the medical community as well as to the public. It is an excellent resource for the most current drug-related discoveries.

Schaffer Library of Drug Policy (www.druglibrary.org/schaffer/index.HTM). This website contains a significant database dedicated to illicit drug research, studies, and government documents.

Serendipity (http://serendipity.magnet.ch/index.html). This website contains hundreds of pages on a wide array of topics. Its index provides links to articles that provide both scientific information and anecdotal accounts of the effects of hallucinogens.

Timothy Leary (www.leary.com/index_top.html). This is the official Timothy Leary website that contains letters, books, speeches, and a few photographs. The site provides insights into Leary's politics as well as spiritual views of hallucinogens.

Urban Legends and Folklore (http://urbanlegends.miningco.com/science/urbanlegends/). This website contains a large number of urban legends categorized by topic, including those dealing with hallucinogen use.

Vaults of Erowid (www.erowid.org/library/books_online/pihkal/pihkal.shtml). This is a comprehensive website that includes the history of illicit drugs, laws governing illicit drugs, religious use of drugs, personal experiences, chemistry, and books.

Index

Picture Credits

Cover photo: Custom Medical Stock Photo, Inc.
Associated Press AP, 67, 72
Associated Press/Fort Worth Star Telegram, 85
© Bettmann/CORBIS, 30, 47
John Chiasson/Getty Images, 80
© Henry Diltz/CORBIS, 12
Chris Felver/Archive Photos, 22
Murray Garrett/Archive Photos, 37
Hulton Getty/Getty Images, 33, 41
John Gress/Getty Images, 61
© R. Konig/Jacana/Photo Researchers, 25
© Ted Kreshinsky/CORBIS, 48
© Larry Mulvehill/Photo Researchers, 56
New York Times Co./Archive Photos, 44
Ron Okiver/Archive Photos, 55
Alfred Pasieka/Science Photo Library/Photo Researchers, 19
PhotoDisc, 77, 83
George Post/Science Photo Library/Photo Researchers, 32
© Reuters NewMedia/CORBIS, 35, 39
Sinclair Stammers/Science Library/Photo Researchers, 43
TEK Image/Science Photo Library/Photo Researchers, 14
U.S. Customs/Getty Images, 62, 90
© Vanni Archive/CORBIS, 27
Jeff Vinnick/Reuters, 88
Alex Wong/Getty Images, 79

About the Author

James Barter received his undergraduate degree in history and classics at the University of California, Berkeley, followed by graduate studies in ancient history and archaeology at the University of Pennsylvania. Mr. Barter has taught history as well as Latin and Greek.

A Fulbright scholar at the American Academy in Rome, Mr. Barter worked on archaeological sites in and around the city as well as on sites in the Naples area. He also has worked and traveled extensively in Greece.

Mr. Barter currently lives in Rancho Santa Fe, California, with his sixteen-year-old daugher Kalista who enjoys soccer, the piano, and mathematics. His older daughter, Tiffany Modell, also lives in Rancho Santa Fe as a violin teacher and music consultant.